THE ELDEST CHILD

THE ELDEST

by EDITH G. NEISSER

HARPER & BROTHERS

CHILD

Author of *Brothers and Sisters*

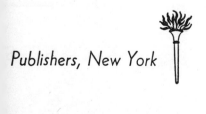

Publishers, New York

THE ELDEST CHILD
Copyright © 1957 by Edith G. Neisser
Printed in the United States of America

FIRST EDITION

H-G

Library of Congress catalog card number: LC 57-11109

18511

To WALTER, *for his understanding*

Contents

Acknowledgments

The ideas, the experiences, and the talents of many different persons were drawn upon in writing this book. Indeed, the generosity with which both strangers and old friends, highly trained professionals and interested amateurs, shared their convictions and gave their assistance was one of the most gratifying aspects of this undertaking.

It is not possible to thank each individual separately here, yet there are a few whose unusual helpfulness I should like to record. The book could not have been written without the critical reading which Dr. Maria W. Piers gave each chapter, nor without the encouragement in its inception of Helen Ross, Administrative Director of the Chicago Institute for Psychoanalysis.

Dr. Mary Langmuir Essex made available the resources of the 1956 Vassar Summer Institute for Parents and Children whose faculty and students contributed interesting and fresh viewpoints.

By tracking down material in the library of Le Centre International de l'Enfance in Paris and by translating the findings of certain research carried on in France, Lisbeth Freschl provided me with data which would otherwise have been inaccessible.

The anthropological material in Chapter I, with the exception of the information on the Japanese, was drawn chiefly from the Human Relations Area Files at the University of Chicago. The Japanese material was gathered in informal conversations with public officials, educators, sociologists, and parents in Tokyo and

Kyoto in the spring of 1956. Dr. Blanche Watrous read Chapter I and clarified and amplified many points out of her own anthropological training and experience.

The staff of the Highland Park Library has been tireless in securing loans of unpublished theses and verifying bibliographical facts. The enthusiastic cooperation of Inger Boye, its children's librarian, greatly facilitated the preparation of the list of books for young people in which a first-born plays a prominent part.

Virginia Dannenbaum and Dorothy Loeb cheerfully typed and retyped the manuscript under considerable pressure.

My husband, Walter Neisser, listened, early and late, to plans, outlines, and revisions and offered suggestions as he read the book at various stages in its development. His patience and understanding have been a constant incentive.

It has been stimulating and rewarding to work with Richard B. McAdoo and Hermine I. Popper as editors, and I am appreciative of their interpretation of the purpose and scope of the book.

EDITH G. NEISSER

Highland Park, Ill.
March 1957.

Prologue

The position of the eldest poses questions that go wide and deep. The first-born has presented one of the persistent perplexities, challenges, and joys of men and women throughout the ages and throughout the earth. Being the first-born child in the family is so strong a force in shaping personality that the position affects the course of an individual's entire life, for better or for worse.

This book has been written because of the expressed concern of parents, teachers, social workers, and doctors about the special problems an eldest must work out. Are these problems inherent in his position or do they result from the way we deal with him? Is our handling of the eldest so firmly imbedded in our customs and traditions that it could not easily be altered? Or could we with more understanding, foresight, and planning decrease some of his difficulties and help him become a healthier, happier personality? If so, what practical steps shall be taken in homes, schools, and informal organizations to accomplish this end?

The position of the eldest today is different in an important way from what it has been through the ages. During and since World War II the fashion in family planning has tended toward having three or four or five children in quick succession. "Might as well stay home with four as with two."

Larger families with children only a year or two apart in age are an old story, but in today's setting these households bear little resemblance to the big family of the nineteenth century. In an earlier America, grandparents, a maiden aunt, a dependent cousin, or paid helpers were likely to augment the household. Houses were roomier, backyards wider, and the empty lot on the corner offered play space when washing on the line crowded the yard.

Now young parents are trying to fit the customs and the values of seventy-five years ago into the ideals and the living arrangements of the present. In this process, praiseworthy as it may be from many angles, the first child in the family is likely to be caught in a difficult and sometimes perilous squeeze.

Choice, as well as the demands of contemporary living, have created a picture of the typical, indeed the happy family as one consisting solely of mother, father, and their children. Space permits only an occasional overnight guest. Budgets allow only semi-occasional sitters or cleaning help.

When necessity has forced young families to move in with grandparents, it has been clearly understood on both sides that this was only a temporary measure. The relative isolation, or the isolation from relatives, in which beginning families elect to live is heightened by grandparents who have busy lives of their own often in distant places. Erstwhile maiden aunts now are gainfully employed and infrequently of a mind to devote their leisure time to nieces or nephews. Unattached uncles, during the years they might make their homes with a married brother or sister, are likely to be serving in the armed forces or being transferred from one branch of a big corporation to another.

Once a disconsolate eldest could find affectionate reassurance in climbing on grandpa's lap or fleeing to the broad bosom of the cook. Such refuges are hard to come by today.

The woebegone two-year-old, who has already been twice deposed by new babies, has no notion of these social and economic forces. He does know that five or six days a week when his mother is occupied with the baby, or the babies, no comforting adult is on hand to tie a shoe lace, find his lost teddy bear, or take his hand and walk down the block. The eldest has some unfinished business to attend to—the business of being a baby himself.

Other groups and other eras have not imposed on young mothers the standards set by the slick advertisements which proclaim that everyone can be radiant, serene, untiring, and efficient, as well as jill-of-all trades by using the proper soap or mop or ice cubes. More than in other countries, and certainly more than in other ages, we in the United States insist that in addition to 'round-the-clock care of several children, plus cooking, cleaning, and washing, a young mother must exert her energy to keep her figure, her husband, and her interest in world affairs. Deep freeze and diaper wash, drip-dry clothes and dishwasher have, we are told (chiefly by those who are not mothers), eased a young woman's lot. Science has not provided any adequate device to make the task of growing up easier for the first-born child in today's families.

It is time, then, that we look at the hazards and the benefits—for benefits there are—that are latent in being the first child today.

The argument might be advanced that everyone has survived having younger brothers and sisters, and even grown to like them. The answer to this reasoning is that a great deal more than survival, either physically or emotionally, is our goal for children. We want to see realized the tremendous potential for enjoyment, for loyalty, and for love that exists between children growing up in the same family.

We know now that chances for experiencing the advantages in being eldest and of developing friendliness toward other children in the family are greater if the inevitable jealousy of the early years of being a brother or sister is not overpowering.

An awareness of both advantages and hazards latent in being eldest provides vital clues to understanding a first-born. Recognizing the favorable and unfavorable possibilities in being the first and for a time the only child, of making room for brothers and sisters, of carrying responsibilities and privileges of seniority, makes it easier to help an eldest take his place in the family and in other groups now and later. With this kind of understanding, parents, teachers, and leaders can more readily supply the guidance and the setting an oldest needs in order to develop into his own best self. How this understanding may be used to solve problems that arise as the eldest or, temporarily, the only boy or girl lives and grows with other persons is the subject of this book.

The questions to consider then become: How can a first-born be given the appropriate chance to work through babyhood so that in time he can leave that phase behind and go on to find satisfaction in being the eldest? How can dealing with the conflicts that his position may bring during childhood and adolescence make him a stronger, better balanced personality?

THE ELDEST CHILD

CHAPTER I

Myth and Custom of the Eldest

Since the beginning of recorded time, in most known societies, the first-born has had special significance. To undersand our own attitudes toward a first child, and to throw them into sharper relief, we need to see them against a background of the ways other peoples and other ages have regarded the eldest. Such a comparison helps to distinguish those feelings toward a first-born that seem to be universal and rooted in human nature from those feelings that are brought about by our own, or by another people's style of life. Then we can contrast the kind of relationships that appear serviceable to us with different solutions. We would not adopt, lock stock and barrel, the customs of another group. Still it is interesting to discover that in other times and other places it has seemed necessary to make special rules to take care of situations we find perplexing.

Examples in this chapter of how other cultures treat the eldest are necessarily only fragments of the numerous influences impinging on a first-born. Yet it is revealing to note what forms the safeguards invoked to protect and honor the eldest have taken, and to consider some of the defenses groups have erected against his supposedly magic powers.

In talking to the Japanese mother of two sons in Tokyo, I discovered how other customs can throw one's own values into better perspective. "Is the oldest son always the favored one? Do you always give him the best of everything from the biggest strawberries to the most thorough education?" was the question. Her answer was, "But of course. Don't you have a favorite who is given the preference in your country?"

When this Japanese mother was asked, "How do the younger ones feel about the oldest brother getting the biggest of whatever is to be divided?," she replied, "The others understand that is the way it is."

"How did your boys get along while they were growing up?" brought forth the characteristic Japanese giggle. "Oh, they fought with each other plenty!"

We take it for granted that equality and fairness are the desirable goals. When we discover that others do not consider them of primary importance, we may wonder, "What do these ways of living together mean to us? Why do we prize them so highly?"

We realize that our way of living in families and communities is based on an ideal, all too often not carried out in practice, that "all men are created equal and are endowed by their creator with certain inalienable rights, that among these are Life, Liberty and . the pursuit of Happiness." Translated into homely terms it means that nobody has a right to the choicest strawberries every day.

Equality is a difficult principle to administer at home, in the neighborhood, or in the nation. In order to be fair each division or dispute, great or small, must be carefully weighed and all its implications considered. What are we trying to instill beyond the immediate incident in our insistence on equality? Is more involved than just a plate of strawberries or its equivalent? One way justice is expressed, for us, is through equality of opportunity in the family, as well as in the wider community. Family customs reflect and reinforce community customs and are, therefore, significant beyond our own front yards.

Among the Laplanders the youngest son inherits the father's reindeer and dwelling. He is expected to take care of his parents in their old age and look after his unmarried sisters. This reversal of the more familiar procedure raises the question as to why so much importance has been attached to being the eldest in many times and places.

FIRST-BORN—THREAT AND PROMISE

When one considers how miraculous and profoundly stirring a first baby is even in today's scientifically sophisticated world, it is small wonder that more naive peoples surrounded a first-born with an aura of magic. The first in any series, whether it be flocks or fruits or children, was highly regarded as the opener of the way in primitive ages. At the same time "first" was equivalent to "dangerous." Among groups which set a higher value on men than on women, a first boy was a greater cause for rejoicing than a first girl. Indeed, when the first-born was a daughter, she might be without special distinction and emphasis was still placed on the first son.

Looking at his first son seems to have brought a man in all times and places the feeling, "Here is one who will carry on after me." In cultures where it is believed a man's security in another life is assured by having descendents to perform the proper ceremonies, this feeling is openly expressed. The sentiment is present in some measure even when, as in our society, a first son has neither such power nor such duties.

From "he will carry on after me" it is but a short step to "he will take my place." To take the place of another meant to supplant him. The arrival of the first son also seemed to foreshadow the father's end. Eldest sons, in some quarters, tended to be a cause for fear as well as rejoicing.

In many parts of the world at various times the first-born was considered so serious a threat to the father's well-being that he was put to death. Among the Uganda in East Africa, if the first child was a boy, he was promptly killed. They believed he would take his father's strength, absorb his father's spirit, and bring about his end. Entering into this twisted thinking was also the idea that the father was born again in his first son. Both could not survive. The father was in a delicate position. Should he live or let his son live? This looked like an "either or" proposition. Since society judged the father to be the more valuable, he lived and the baby was killed.

In Polynesia, particularly in Tahiti until recent times, the idea that the father was reborn in the son was also held, but a less destructive solution to the dilemma was found. A king or a noble would abdicate in favor of his infant son and rule as regent. In abdicating, the father relinquished his honors and possessions to the baby. If a man was not willing to step aside, he had no choice but to kill his son. Frequently, fathers did just that.

Some groups believed that on reaching manhood, sons became their fathers' equals. Fiji Islanders required a boy who was judged grown up to wrestle with his father. If the boy won, he would forcibly take possession of the family farm.

A son of the chief of the Corannas, a South African tribe, would in a not distant past, sit in the hut drinking milk so that he would grow strong. When he became a man, the father brought him two short sticks. Father and son fought with these sticks. If the younger won, he became leader of the kraal.

A SACRIFICE TO THE GODS

When the Israelites came into Canaan, they found the inhabitants making burnt offerings of their children on the altars of Moloch, that symbol of evil frequently mentioned in the Old Testament. The Phoenicians practiced similar rites and usually, it appears, the eldest son or daughter was the victim. Surrounded by peoples who customarily made burnt offerings of their eldest children, the ancient Israelites of the Biblical period from time to time forsook the doctrines and the high principled conduct counseled by their leaders and, going back to what may have been earlier practices of their own, copied their idolatrous and inhuman neighbors.

Micah was posing a question that puzzled people in his day when in the sixth chapter of the book bearing his name in the Bible he asks, "Wherewith shall I come before the Lord and bow myself before the High God? Shall I give my first born for my transgression?"

It is almost incredible that men and women who could seriously consider killing their eldests could also grasp the ethic that Micah gives them in the next verse, for his own answer to the query is an ideal we are still far from reaching. "He hath showed thee, O man, what is good and what doth the Lord require of thee, but to do justly, to love mercy and walk humbly with the Lord thy God."

Sir James Frazer in *The Golden Bough* (N.Y., Macmillan, 1935) tells us that ancient Chinese history speaks of a state where it was customary to devour the first-born son. As part of a religious ceremony, the aboriginal tribes of New South Wales ate the first child to be born to a family. In pre-Christian times in Ireland "firstlings" of the flocks and herds, and also the first son of the chief of the clan, were offered as sacrifices to insure successful crops. In pre-Christian Russia and among some tribes in southern Abyssinia, the same custom prevailed. The sacrifice of the first child was believed necessary to protect the health and prosperity of the entire family among one tribe of Indians in British Columbia. Another nearby tribe offered the first-born to the sun god. Among the Sabines, a dominant group in Italy before the founding of Rome, a great spring festival involved the sacrifice of the first-born.

When Xerxes marched from Persia through Thessaly to attack the Spartans in the fifth century B.C. he was shown the statue at Aulus where it had formerly been the custom to sacrifice the king's eldest son to one of the deities of ancient Greece. Later a ram was substituted for the baby boy. As long as the prince stayed out of the city and did not remind the god of his existence he was safe.

This recalls legends and fairy tales about the nobly born baby who is left exposed in a remote forest or on a mountain top. He is supposed to die, but usually some herdsman or wood cutter cares for him. These stories are believed to have their origin in that dim past of the human race when this subterfuge was the only escape from a vengeful spirit for a first male child.

As late as the beginning of the nineteenth century, first children in India were often sacrificed to the sacred river Ganges.

Whether it was in Abyssinia or British Columbia, pre-historic

Ireland or New South Wales, these were apparently violent tribes who attributed an extreme blood thirstiness to their gods as well as fearing the magic power of a "first." To placate them, the most precious thing in the world must be offered, and then, as now, what is more precious than the first child? Clearly, the first child as an extraordinary creature has been a part of human nature since families began to exist.

THE SUN NEVER SETS ON THE PRESTIGE OF THE ELDEST

While our concern is primarily with the eldest's position in his family during childhood, it is useful to know something about the honors that will be his when he is grown. We may safely assume that one who is to hold a high and sacred trust in later life will also be set apart in his early days for special consideration.

The custom of primogeniture, making the eldest the successor to the rights and the property of either or both parents, is not a primitive practice, though it is done in many nonliterate tribes. Any group that establishes the principle of undivided inheritance must have reached the stage of having family property to conserve.

Primogeniture may be rooted in the mystical belief in the importance of first fruits, as was the case among the people of the Old Testament, but there is a practical side to it, too. In the powerful monarchies of the ancient East, as well as in the royal houses of Europe in recent centuries, making the direct line of succession from eldest son to eldest son (or as in England, from first-born to first-born, be it son or daughter) kept intact and strengthened central government.

Among the aristocracy and the common people as well as among royalty, the eldest, and generally the eldest son, has been the heir in Oriental countries, among many African tribes, and frequently, but not invariably, in Europe. By written or sometimes unwritten law, house and lands were the portion of the first-born. The man of property who makes a will is the exception rather than the rule in many cultures. If the father dies without a will, the eldest son is the unquestioned heir in some parts of the world.

The colonial lawmakers in America felt something should be

done to give eldest sons the lion's share of the inheritance. By borrowing from the English common law of a much earlier day, various complex laws for inheritance were set up in the several colonies conferring special benefits on the first-born son. After the Revolutionary War these benefits were abolished. This came about not because the practices were undemocratic but because they were found not to be serviceable in a frontier economy.

How strong has been the tradition of handing on property to the eldest is illustrated by the situation in Japan. The 1946 constitution decreed that property should be divided among the sons and daughters of the family at the death of the father. Before that, the eldest son had inherited house and lands, cared for aged parents, and assisted brothers and sisters. Today the oldest Japanese son still has the burdens, but neither the authority nor the relative wealth. In many villages with the connivance of the local officials, families have returned to the old plan.

There is a certain logic in making the eldest the heir. Some of his prestige has derived from his being the one who will someday possess the family's wealth, whatever it may be. The eldest will have more time to learn and to mature before his father dies. For economic reasons also it is sensible to pass on property undivided.

In Dahomey, on the Gulf of Guinea in West Africa, inheritance has a different twist. Primogeniture prevails, but the youngest is believed to inherit greater wisdom. The theory is that parents grow wiser with age, and therefore the youngest has the richest inheritance in that respect.

THE FAMILY PRIEST

When the first-born were no longer sacrificed on the altars of the local gods they often became the ones considered most suited to approach the tribal deities. Their life rather than their death became a dedication to whatever powers or ancestral spirits must be served. This priesthood took a variety of forms.

Among the Thonga, a tribe of Bantu people in Africa, there is no priestly caste. Each family makes its offering to the gods on an individual basis, with the eldest brother officiating. Anyone wishing to approach the gods with a request must do so through the eldest son of the oldest living generation. If a younger brother quarrels with the oldest one, who had become the intermediary with the supernatural forces, and they take an oath not to see each other, the younger is in effect excommunicated. In case it were necessary for the younger one to make a prayer or an offering, in an epidemic or in some other dire emergency, he would first need to become reconciled to his eldest brother. To attempt to take the place of the eldest would bring down on one's head a divine wrath so intense that it might result in death.

The Azande, who live in the southern part of the Sudan, decree that the eldest of the oldest generation alive is the priest in the family. He carries out the family rites in honor of the spirits of the dead. When a man builds a shrine for the ancestral spirits in his hut, the eldest brother performs certain ceremonies.

In feudal China and under the Empire, the eldest son enjoyed a privileged position as the future head of the family who would officiate in ancestor worship. Through him the life of the family was transmitted. In Korea, and also in Vietnam, the eldest son became the family's high priest. The peace and honor of the ancestors rested on the shoulders of the eldest sons in Shinto households in Japan.

THE ELDEST MUST BE A LEARNED MAN

In some cultures notably in China, in Central Europe and in Italy, the special importance of the eldest son was marked by giving him educational advantages, even though the rest of the family must make financial sacrifices to do so. As a result, there was heavy pressure on him to be successful. Among Jewish groups there has always been the hope that the eldest son would become a man of learning. Mothers bent every effort to see this dream realized. Many first and second generation Italian, Polish, and Jewish families have carried on their ideal of special educational advantages for the eldest son.

AN AWESOME FIGURE TO THE YOUNGER ONES

Seniority is also honored through rules about the way younger brothers and sisters treat the eldest. In northern Nigeria, among the Tiv, the eldest brother is treated with such respect by his juniors that they are not permitted to address him with the expressions ordinarily used by young people when they talk together. The eldest sister in Korea must be addressed respectfully by younger members of the family, too.

Our own eldest might well envy their counterparts among the Chaga in Africa. The younger children are forbidden to quarrel with the eldest who may order them around. They may not accuse him or berate him in any way. An insult to the eldest son is an insult to the father. An insult to the eldest daughter is an insult to the mother.

In Japan, the younger children looked with awe on their oldest brother who was deferred to even by the mother because he would be head of the family when the father died.

In China before the changes of the last twenty-five years, when the father died and the eldest son succeeded to the honors and obligations of the head of the family, his friendly, easy-going relationship with his younger brothers changed abruptly. He became, much to the discomfiture of his juniors, the authoritarian ruler of the household.

In Afghanistan when a father dies the house is taken over by the eldest son. Like the eldest brother in many cultures in Africa, in Europe, in the Orient, and among some American Indian tribes, he must give his widowed mother and his sisters, both married and unmarried, shelter and counsel. The Aleutian Islanders say, "If one does not have a father, then in his place one must honor one's elder brother and obey him like a father."

The eldest son confers honor on his mother in India. Among the African Chaga the eldest son is the mother's favorite because he is the one who has given her a position in her husband's family.

DOES HONOR SPOIL HIM?

What does it do to a person who as he is growing up is steadily deferred to? In *A Daughter of the Samurai* (Garden City, Doubleday, 1925), an autobiography by Etsu Sugimoto, the author, who grew up in a Japanese family where feudal traditions were strong, describes her eldest brother as a discontented, disaffected individual. Apparently, this is no isolated instance of the eldest son turning out to be a misfit. The Mayor of Kyoto related to me that the Japanese have a proverb, "The eldest son is an incompetent." Everything, Mr. Takayama explained, was made so easy for the eldest boy in former times that he had no challenge to meet.

When the eldest was not equal to his responsibilities the second son took over. Those who have observed Japanese families through the years report that second sons are often the ones who, in actual practice, are looked to as the family's head when the father dies. A second son, whose mother lives with him today, explains that he has this honor only because his elder brother is out of the country on business. The explanation takes on additional meaning in the light of the proverbially irresponsible conduct of the eldest.

This pattern is quite contrary to our picture of an eldest. Although occasionally in our society we do encounter a first-born son, followed in the family by several girls, who is too much adored by his mother and sisters. When he grows up and finds life outside his home not so agreeable he retreats to being looked after by his women folk.

DEPUTY-DISCIPLINARIANS

A first-born boy or a girl is valued because he will be an economic asset and a real help almost as soon as he, or more particularly she, can get around independently and follow a simple direction.

Taking care of the younger children is not always the task of the eldest daughter alone, however. Eldest boys are sometimes called upon to perform those duties also. From the Navaho Indians to the Ashanti, an inland people of West Africa, from the Orient to Central Europe, the eldest carries real responsibility for younger brothers and sisters. Five- and six-year-olds in many parts of the world have one baby strapped on their backs and are leading another by the hand. Amazingly enough, the older ones still seem able to play and the babies do not protest, but this responsibility often affects unfavorably the children's relationship with one another.

WHEN THE ELDEST IS A SORCERER

There are at least two localities where witch-like evil powers are attributed to the eldest girl. The accusations are so well-defined a part of the culture that a conspicuous absence of good will between the youthful supervisor and her charges is evident.

The eldest Navaho daughter has a special place in the family. She takes over the younger children as they are weaned. Even when she herself is no more than a yard child of four or five she becomes the nurse of the second, the knee baby, when that one is displaced by a third arrival. This assignment is fraught with difficulties and dangers for her.

A Navaho infant is the center of attraction. His mother gratifies his wishes without delay. Then with no warning comes an abrupt weaning. No longer the darling of the family, he is turned over to the oldest sister. She had suffered a similar deprivation on the arrival of this baby not so long ago. Naturally, she has a reservoir of resentment toward the erstwhile baby of the family.

To make matters worse, the small nurse gets the brunt of her charge's rage. Navaho custom prohibits showing anger to one's mother or a baby, but there are no prohibitions against being angry at a sister. These clashing interests hardly make for camaraderie between children in the family. Yet the eldest girl must teach her younger brothers and sisters as they are weaned and come under her care the manners and the techniques they need in order to get along in the tribe.

If one or more of the younger children should die, the suspicion of witchcraft would be strong and would fall upon the eldest daughter. Perhaps this kind of suspicion may have resulted from the unbearable tension between the oldest sister and the younger children, for no love is lost between the oldest sister and the smaller ones for whom she is accountable. Those who originally imputed evil powers to the unfortunate girls may have had dim memories of what they thought their own oldest sisters were doing to them when they were small.

A small child often daydreams about inflicting, or fears he has inflicted, an injury on a brother or sister with whom he is angry. We take pains to make it clear to our children that his wishes and his words harm no one. Even with such reassurance, our children are often worried about their bad thoughts. Imagine how weighted down with fear and guilt a girl must be if the beliefs of the adults around her give support to her own worst fears about her capacity to do harm. No wonder the relationship between the child-nurse and her charges is the wellspring of lifelong bitterness in this tribe.

In the highlands of Guatemala, in the village of San Pedrola la Laguna, a similar kind of sorcery is attributed to the eldest child. If several younger children in the family die in infancy, the eldest is suspected of surviving by consuming their spirits. When this happens an elaborate curing rite is invoked on the birth of the next baby in the family, to put an end to the eldest's baleful magic. A midwife or a man skilled in supernatural arts is called in. A chicken, preferably black, and of the same gender as the child is selected. Chicken, child and curer must be of the same sex.

The offending child is beaten on the back with the chicken. Then the chicken is killed, cooked, and fed to the child who must eat it all, even though it takes him several sittings to do so. While the luckless culprit eats, he or she is told, "Now that little brother or sister is here, you must take good care of him and never frighten him. This chicken is like his flesh." If the child eats the chicken with a good appetite, his desire to consume the baby's spirit is supposedly put at rest. If he eats reluctantly, and that chicken might well have the taste of dust and ashes, then he or she may still be dangerous.

HUMAN NATURE VS. CUSTOM AND TRADITION

Around the world there seem to be three features common to the lot of eldest children. When the next baby is nursed, they show their resentment by petulance, temper tantrums, and other kinds of disturbances familiar in our own homes. The way a child expresses his protest varies with what the customs in his community and the atmosphere in his home will permit.

A revealing illustration by a research worker is presented in a French journal describing a case of a three-year-old's relation to his newborn sister. Basically, the point of view and the phrasing in the French report are the same as would be found in a similar discussion in a professional journal in the United States. Yet in describing the boy's behavior, the author says, "He had previously been a sweet, compliant child. He now has temper tantrums and stamps his foot when he is scolded." Stamping his foot when he is scolded seems like a mild protest for a three-year-old boy, in comparison with the way outraged youngsters of that age would act in the United States. Trained observers have pointed out that French children tend to be gentler. Here is one of those slight, but significant, differences which point up how responses are modulated by the general tone of the environment. Still, whenever a mother has more than one child in her exclusive care there seems to be tension between the children.

A second varying, but universal, custom is that the eldest is expected to take responsibility for younger brothers and sisters. The amount of responsibility ranges from the complete care assigned a Navaho girl to the intermittent and partial watching out for younger ones that is expected of middle-class children in the United States or England.

Finally, the eldest seems to be in some degree "special," though that specialness is manifested in widely different kinds of treatment. The effect on the eldest of his resentment and his responsibilities differs from one culture to another, as well as among individuals within a given group. In some groups the eldest tends to become a leader and a stable, dependable individual. In others, the characteristic behavior of the first-born is to evade responsibility. In some groups solidarity tends to develop between the children in the family. Elsewhere, there is conspicuous distrust and the condition prevails as described in the African proverb, "They hate like brothers."

The fact that jealousy is present seems to be universal. Not that fact, but the way it is handled makes the difference between its being a corroding, embittering experience or one that furthers the development of personality.

The specialness with which the eldest is regarded is so general as to be basic to human nature; yet each culture gives its eldests its own form of distinction. A fundamental tenet of child rearing —that each child is different—operates in every known society. Nowhere does everyone fit into the same mould, but there are still characteristic ways of behaving that distinguish each group, even though individuals within it differ among themselves.

MYTHS ARE A KEY TO FEELINGS

In addition to what we can learn by contrasting some of our attitudes with those of other cultures, folk-tales and myths reveal how the eldest has been regarded in other times and places and may throw further light on sentiments of our own. Clyde Kluck-hohn and Dorothea Leighton in *The Navaho* (Cambridge, Harvard University Press, 1946) explain that

Folk-lore must be presumed to originate in the dreams and phantasies of individuals, but when the product of one person's imagination (as mingled with and modified by the phantasy of other persons over a long period of time) is taken over as a part of the mythology of a whole group, the themes may confidently be assumed to correspond to widely current psychological situations.

In other words, where there is the smoke of oft-repeated situations in stories, we may suppose that there is the fire of actual practice or actual feelings among those who tell the tales. Cain's jealousy of Abel is pretty strong evidence that rivalry between brothers for the favor of the father goes back as far as family life itself.

The Oedipus myth, source of so much drama and poetry, relates how Laius, king of Thebes, was warned by an oracle that his newborn first son would be a peril to his life and his throne. The baby was therefore taken to a mountain side and left to die. A shepherd found him and brought him to the King of Corinth, who called him Oedipus and raised him as his own son. As a young man, Oedipus learned through an oracle that he would be the death of his father. Believing the King of Corinth was his father, he attempted to escape his fate by fleeing the city. On the road, he encountered his real parent, became involved in an argument with him, and killed him. Sometime later Oedipus turned up in Thebes, rid that city of the Sphinx, and as a reward was given the queen, whom he did not know was his mother, as his wife by the grateful Thebans. When famine and pestilence came to Thebes, an oracle revealed the Queen's relation to Oedipus and unmitigated tragedy resulted on all sides.

Here again is the fear that a first-born son will supplant his father. In this story, too, the son takes his father's place—a reflection of a deeply rooted wish, as well as a fear, on the son's part.

In the epics of ancient India, the Vedas, the eldest had special privileges reserved for him. He was like the father, and was to be honored and to receive the largest share of the inheritance. Often the stories of the Vedas centered around conflicts over the father's property. The highest virtue was brotherly love. The epics tell of magic formulae and hymns to be repeated to attain this virtue.

Navaho myths are often concerned with family situations. The despised child is the hero and overcomes the child who has been indulged. (How Cinderella does get around!) The witch or the werewolf of Navaho legends turns out to be a brother or sister, while witches and similar unsavory characters in other cultures turn out to be fathers, grandfathers, or in general figures of an awe-inspiring nature. Here again is an indication of the strong resentment Navaho children harbor both toward those who have come after them or those who have preceded them in the family.

The witch stories give an expression to feelings which, among the Navaho, must be suppressed. One reason for the survival of the myths is undoubtedly that they have been a means of getting feelings about brothers and sisters, in indirect fashion, into words. By letting children know that others have had the same anxieties they have, the myths have probably also lightened the youngster's fear of being found out and punished.

WHAT REPORT OF THE ELDEST IN FAIRY TALES?

The fairy tales and many of the old familiar stories have been retold from place to place and handed on from generation to generation, undergoing variations as they were passed along. Wherever one searches, the eldest gives a poor account of himself. No Little Man in pointed cap appears to succor eldest brothers. No fairy waves her wand for an eldest sister, except to get her deeper into difficulties.

As an example, take Perrault's *Puss in Boots,* (N.Y., Scribners, 1952). In the opening lines of the story the eldest son receives the father's mill, the second the ass, and the third nothing but the cat. Yet what amazing feats that cat performed for its master!

The eldest, or the two older (the magic number three is the usual rule for family size in fairy tales) may start out well endowed but the oldest manages to waste his substance or to be outdone by the youngest.

The eldest in a fairy story runs the gamut of disagreeableness from scheming, proud, and crafty to ugly, cruel, and wicked. At best the eldest is stuffy and priggish. James R. Foster, author of *The World's Great Folk Tales* (N. Y., Harper, 1953) and *Great Folk Tales of Wit and Humor* (N. Y., Harper, 1955) said to me in a letter, "I have read thousands of folk-tales and I cannot remember one in which, if there are several brothers and sisters in the dramatis personae, the eldest is treated sympathetically."

WHY IS THE ELDEST THE VILLAIN?

Clearly, the exigencies of dramatic climax make it more desirable to have the first two, or four, or six brothers or sisters fall short so that a happy finale with the youngest, the victor, can end the suspense. Yet the demands of plot structure alone cannot account for the bad light in which fairy tales place the eldest. W. R. S. Ralston in his *Russian Fairy Tales* (Smith and Elder, 1873) says that the older brothers in the stories are the sons of an earlier, displaced queen. They hate the youngest because his mother has supplanted their mother in the father's affections. The father is usually a king. The older ones want to get rid of the youngest, and in that role they are necessarily crafty, cruel and generally a bad lot.

The cleverness of the youngest in these stories has a parallel in the folk tales about animals. In West African folklore, the trickster is always the small, weak, despised creature who must necessarily live by its wits. Nearer home, B'rer Rabbit and the Sly Mongoose of Jamaican lore get the best of their bigger, stronger brothers in the world of beasts. That favorite of three generations, Peter Rabbit, is another eldest who came to grief, while Flopsy, Mopsy, and Cottontail were "good little bunnies and had bread and milk and blackberries for supper."

Richard Church, in *Over the Bridge* (N.Y., Dutton, 1956) voices the feeling many younger children have about elder or eldest brothers or sisters. "I knew, however, that Jack . . . would accuse me of showing off or of creating a scene. He had a horror of any form of demonstration, and he discouraged extravagance and self-indulgence, two weaknesses which he was always prepared to detect in me and to correct." Perhaps these fairy stories, like the Navaho legends, give an expression to the feelings brothers and sisters have had about the eldest through the ages.

The eldest brother or sister does not offer the comfort or security a mother or a father or another trusted adult might, but still he is vested with the right to order younger ones around. Looked at from the lower rungs of the family ladder, the position of the eldest is one identified with authority, yet not carrying the real strength of authority.

FICTION TREATS THE ELDEST BETTER

Fairy tales may follow in the main a stereotype, but novels, short stories, plays, and even poetic drama portray a wide range of eldest brothers and sisters. Fiction and drama are drawn from life and so have as rich a variety of eldests as life itself. You can find eldest brothers all the way from Tom Tulliver in George

Eliot's *Mill on the Floss,* who tormented and exploited his younger sister, expecting everything and giving nothing in return, to the central figure in J. D. Salinger's *Catcher in the Rye,* who adored his little sister and found in her the one stabilizing force in his life. You can find eldest sisters who are kindly, responsible, and competent like Meg in *Little Women* or who are possessive, domineering, and unbearably self-righteous like Alice in Rebecca West's *Salt of the Earth.* There are as many shades of generosity and protectiveness, selfishness and bad temper, in fiction as you can observe around you in twenty years. A list of reading in which eldests play a prominent role is to be found at the end of this book.

Since the dawn of family life, the first-born has been an individual of special importance. Sometimes he has been invested with a magic power regarded as dangerous, but more often he has been honored and given the best the family had to offer. In some cultures, the responsibilities thrust upon him in childhood or in adulthood have made his life a hard one, in spite of the privileges accorded to him. In other times and places everything has been done to smooth the way for him.

In America today we still tend to confer some benefits on him; but they are likely to be intangible—a matter more of attitudes than of definite privileges. Responsibilities are far less clearly defined by law or custom than they have been in other ages and other cultures. We think about not placing undue burdens on him and are inclined to play down his or her traditional specialness.

Against this background, we can consider how the adults in his life can help an eldest profit from each phase of growing up and make the most of his innate strengths. We can examine the interplay of external and internal forces which shape his feelings about himself and those around him. As a result of such understanding on the part of those who live with him and teach him, the first-born may more often find his position a fortunate one.

CHAPTER II

The First Child Creates a
New Family

As a man and wife start on parenthood and meet the untried situations it presents, their attitude toward their first child is many-faceted. If anyone were to ask either of them how he or she felt toward that baby, the answer would undoubtedly be, "I love him. What do you expect?" Yet looked at closely, feelings are not made out of whole cloth. They are more like a patchwork quilt in which the patches are remnants of early experiences in one's own family. A flowered print may clash with the striped material next to it on the patchwork bedspread, but both contribute to the over-all pattern. Just so conflicting feelings exist in the best of parents. Devotion and irritation, enjoyment and weariness, eagerness and hesitancy can be present at almost the same moment. The patchwork simile breaks down here, for a piece of cloth is static, while feelings shift and vary. As they do so, they pull us emotionally this way and that. This two-way pull is one of the principal driving forces in our behavior.

Some of the forces shaping attitudes toward a first child are a mother's or father's position in his or her own family, relations to brothers and sisters in younger days, circumstances in the parents' own lives at the moment, and their relationship to each other. Whether the baby is of the sex that was wished for may affect feelings about him.

No matter how far we think we have removed ourselves from older traditions, no matter how insistent we are that "just so it's a healthy baby, who cares whether it's a boy or a girl," each of us probably has a slight preference. There is in many circles a lingering notion that "it's fine if the first one is a boy." A girl born into a family that deeply wanted the eldest to be a son may have a shade less eager welcome. Baby girls have their own ways of charming their parents, and parental disappointment usually vanishes soon. Still, it may influence the innermost feelings of a mother or father toward this child.

If a daughter was looked for and a son arrives, a mother may sigh regretfully as she resigns herself to buying blue jeans and corduroys instead of smocked batiste and starched ruffles.

HISTORY NEED NOT REPEAT ITSELF

The idea that family history will necessarily repeat itself has a strong hold. This legend is made credible by the fact that the younger generation seems to follow in the footsteps of its predecessors more closely and more frequently than mere chance would dictate. One reason for similarity in behavior within the wider family group is that mothers and fathers are afraid that a child—particularly the eldest—will show certain undesirable family traits. Without being aware of what is happening, the parent sets the stage and virtually coaches the players to reenact the drama played out in the previous generation.

If there has been a black sheep in the family, or a roving relative who was always about to discover a diamond mine, a mother or father may worry lest their eldest take after this uncle or grandfather. In an effort to curb any latent tendencies toward alibiing, or idleness, or whatever may be suspected of presaging nonconformity, parents may be especially stern. The natural heedlessness of a seven- or nine- or eleven-year-old boy may be looked upon as evidence that he is following in the footsteps of the dubious relative.

One father, whose wife's brother had been irresponsible and a burden, said of his ten-year-old son who sometimes forgot his manners or neglected his homework, "With all this grief on his mother's side, our boy's got two strikes against him before he starts. He must be made to toe the mark."

The boy certainly had two strikes against him, but they were not the ones his father supposed. His mother's and father's lack of confidence in him could do more damage than a dozen ne'er-do-well uncles. A child tends to conform to the picture others have of him and the picture he acquires of himself. That picture is often a mother's or father's memory of a brother or sister.

A first child may remind a parent of the eldest in his own family. The remark of one father when he looked at his newborn daughter was, "I sure hope she won't have a disposition like her Aunt Margaret's."

This man claimed that he had been "bossed to death" by his eldest sister. As his daughter grew out of babyhood, he was unnecessarily hard on her when she showed signs of healthy self-assertion.

The little girl did look like her aunt, for biological heredity often makes for similarity in appearance in succeeding generations. The handing on of personality traits is a far different story. Those who have studied families explain that the blood-will-tell attitude of parents often brings about in the younger generation a repetition of qualities not accounted for by proven principles of heredity. Mannerisms and characteristic responses are caught early in life, but these resemblances between members of the two generations are due to contagion, not heredity. Hopes and fears may make a parent unduly sensitive to entirely normal behavior in a son or daughter if it reminds him of something he disliked in a brother or sister.

Self-assertion is part of a two-year-old's development, just as a certain amount of carelessness is to be expected in a ten-year-old. Helping a child grow out of such typically childish behavior is more effective than scolding or punishing him for it. Harsh measures to stamp out a particular kind of behavior on the ground that it is evidence of hereditary weakness may only serve to emphasize it, make it more intense and harder to outgrow.

If a child's picture of himself is "I have a bad disposition" or "I am lazy"; or if any other undesirable trait is highlighted, the child will tend increasingly to conform to that image.

Adults outside the immediate family who are acquainted with a child's background, as well as parents, sometimes over-react to qualities they believe are evidence of inherited weaknesses. A parent, a teacher, or anyone else in charge of a youngster might test himself with the question, "If I did not know that other members of this child's family had these faults, would I be so alarmed?" The answer can often lead to a more equable way of dealing with the child and a truer estimate of his personality.

An honest effort not to prejudge a youngster or be prejudiced against him because of unsettled scores with their own brothers and sisters in earlier days may clarify some issues for parents. Every child has the right to develop into his own best self. Expecting him to fit into a mould, and a lopsided one at that, can cramp his development.

PLEASANT ASSOCIATIONS PERSIST, TOO

Memories of an eldest brother or sister are often of a happier sort. The aura that surrounded an eldest sister who was a protector and a confidante, an eldest brother who was a hero, may be transferred to one's own first child. This is especially likely to happen if the first-born is of the same sex as the eldest who was beloved. Resemblance by contagion can be a constructive force, but more's the pity, it usually goes unrecognized when it is an aid to sound development.

A parent who has been the eldest in his own family, tends to see himself in the first-born. The desire to win for this child the same kind of pleasant experiences, as well as to protect a first son or daughter from aspects of the position which proved distasteful, is sometimes conscious and sometimes unconscious. There may be an especially close bond all through life between the parent who was an eldest and this first child. The closeness is likely to be intensified if the parent and the child in question are of the same sex. A father who enjoyed considerable prestige as the eldest may, without being aware of it, try to arrange matters so that his eldest son also is the favored one. If the father does not carry this so far that he wants the son to make up for his own shortcomings or carry out ambitions he could not realize, both the father's and son's lives may be enriched by this close tie. Nor do other children in the family, in spite of minor jealousies, invariably suffer because of a slight degree of favoritism for the eldest.

A mother who feels that too much was demanded of her in the way of looking after the younger children, doing the housework, and renouncing her own interests, may insist that her eldest daughter or son will never be burdened in similar fashion. She may bend over backwards not to ask this boy or girl to stop playing in order to do errands or keep an eye on younger brothers and sisters.

Another frequent attitude, spoken or unspoken, on the part of parents who themselves were the eldest is: "I had to give in to my younger sister, and it never hurt me any," or "I spent my Saturdays helping my mother with the washing and cleaning, and I expect my oldest girl to do the same thing." Sometimes there is an unconscious, but pardonable, resentment on the part of such a parent that his own first child is escaping certain hardships or inconveniences. In that case, instead of the similarity in position drawing parent and child closer, it becomes a source of contention.

Parents who have been the first in their own families from time to time probably have their relationship with their eldest colored to a slight degree by each of these attitudes. That is all to the good, for a steady emphasis on either one would make for an imbalance. Nobody can get away entirely from seeing himself in his children, especially in the child who occupies a similar position in the family, yet parents can keep in mind that here is an individual facing different problems. He has different equipment for meeting them.

WHEN A BABY BECOMES A RIVAL

Frequently one who has been the eldest in an exceptionally large family finds himself resenting his first baby. His most persistent early memories center around his mother bathing babies, feeding babies, playing with babies. When he looks back on his childhood it seems that when he needed his mother most he was told, "Don't bother me right now. Can't you see I'm busy with the baby?" One such man still harbored memories of the bicycle denied him because another baby was on the way, and the whole family felt the pinch of strained circumstances. The ball games he missed because he was summoned as an unwilling baby-tender were still a source of irritation.

For several months this young man had felt guilty about his vague distaste for his infant son. Then one evening he came home and called to his wife. When he heard her answer, "Just a minute 'til I finish with the baby," old scenes flashed across his mind. "This is where I came in," he exploded, half angry at the baby and half annoyed at himself for being, as he now realized, so unreasonably childish.

Understanding the source of a feeling does not make it evaporate, but it may reduce resentment to manageable proportions. This father never became a great admirer of babies, but at least he transferred less often his annoyance at his own small sisters to his child. As another son and daughter came along, he saw to it that his eldest had a full share of attention. When there was any question of the eldest giving up some treat or some privilege for the younger ones, the father was his staunch champion.

That an adult can be jealous of a small baby is not altogether reasonable, but the feelings of even well balanced adults are not consistent and mature on every occasion.

Inconsistent feelings may lie much deeper, as was the case with Mrs. Davies. She had had three older sisters. All four girls were bright and attractive. The pace of life was swift in her childhood home. Vera Davies' parents were ambitious for their daughters and saw to it that the girls had what are often described as "advantages"—all the extra lessons, clubs, trips, and excursions that could be crammed into the week. Competition among the sisters was friendly on the surface, but intense.

As the youngest, Vera was always scrambling to keep up. She zealously defended her place in her mother's and father's affections. Her possessions, her clothes, and as she grew up, her friends were guarded carefully from her sisters' raids. It seemed to Vera that her sisters might at any moment snatch away what she treasured most. Small wonder that Vera was as possessive about her husband, Peter, as she was happy in her marriage.

When Peter and Vera's first baby came, grandparents and aunts agreed that Joy was the prettiest of the grand-daughters. For a time, Vera basked in the glory of having an extraordinarily appealing baby. Peter adored his daughter and was deft in caring for her. At first this added to Vera's pleasure in the baby, but before long she began to insist that Joy was being spoiled. Peter, she declared, was making too much fuss over the little girl.

When Joy could pull herself up and walk around, Vera became strict about not allowing her to become "one of those dreadful children who handles everything and always wants her own way." The young mother set high standards of good behavior. Joy was never quite quick enough, neat enough, or sufficiently self-controlled to satisfy her mother. Try as she might, poor Joy was frequently in disgrace. A brother who was born when Joy was two was dealt with far more leniently.

A girl who despairs of pleasing her mother finds the real world hard. Only in her daydreams could Joy savor success, and she retreated there increasingly. Peter accepted Vera's notions about Joy's upbringing, but he still gave the little girl his affectionate companionship. That was a comfort to her, but it could not rescue her from all her difficulties. When she was in fifth grade her inability to concentrate brought her to the attention of the school counselor.

Because Joy lived in a community where child guidance services were available and because her parents sincerely wanted to help her, they followed the counselor's recommendation and took Joy to the child guidance clinic. After many months of weekly sessions, Joy began to gain confidence in herself. She was able to keep a better balance between tasks that must be performed and daydreams about what she wished would happen. Real life became less disagreeable, for her mother's severity relaxed, too.

Interviews with a member of the clinic staff were opening Mrs. Davies' eyes to those feelings from the past which had influenced her relationship with Joy. She was helped to realize that she would have been inclined to be a perfectionist anyway for she clung to the traditions of her own parents. Then she had been disappointed because Joy was a girl. Her life-long rivalry with her sisters made her uneasy about sharing her husband's attention even with her own baby. Mrs. Davies had been both pleased with Joy and somewhat resentful of her, although she would not have been able to put her feelings into words.

Mrs. Davies could see after her talks with the clinic staff member that the more pressure she had put on Joy as the little girl grew up, the clumsier, the more hesitant, the more withdrawn Joy had become, and the more the girl had provoked her. Here was a vicious circle that spelled a strained relationship between mother and daughter. A combination of circumstances, not just one cause or one incident, created the strain. It is reassuring to remember that persistent, repeated difficulties, not the occasional disappointment or punishment, make the deep impression on a child. The elasticity of the human spirit is a strong ally of emotional well-being.

Fortunately, two parents have different feelings about their first child. Memories or ambitions may create some adverse attitudes in one parent, but the other usually has different sentiments on those points. A child's personality is shaped by both the favorable and the unfavorable attitudes of his mother and of his father. Contrasting feelings tend to counterbalance each other and keep things on an even keel. "Counterbalance" does not mean "wipe out." The warmth and kindliness Joy received from her father had not canceled the effects of her mother's unreasonableness, but it had been a saving grace, for it created the groundwork on which Joy, with the help of the child guidance clinic, could build better ways of dealing with her everyday world.

NONEXISTENT BROTHERS AND SISTERS MAY BE A FORCE

It might be supposed that a parent who had been an only child would arrive at motherhood or fatherhood unencumbered by the emotional baggage which has been discussed here. Human beings are so complicated that the brother or sister one never had can be as poignant a memory and as strong an influence as a physical presence. A mother who as a child longed for a sister may see in her first-born girl the companion she always wanted. Under a happy combination of circumstances, the daughter may benefit by a double dose of love, for she receives both what is a daughter's due and what the mother had to give as a sister.

Yet there are dangers in such a relationship. A mother, just because she feels that she has a sister in her little girl, may compete with her. When the daughter reaches adolescence, the usual, and quite normal, conflict between the two generations may be intensified to an unpleasant pitch. In general a relationship between members of two generations does most to promote healthy personality and brings the greatest satisfactions when both individuals concerned are able and willing to act their age, in every sense of that useful phrase.

One mother who had been an only child found it difficult to give her small son the steadying discipline he needed. She had been a timid little girl, rather afraid of boys and what she had been taught to regard as their rough ways. Her first child was an active boy who from babyhood moved with the speed of lightning. In addition to her timidity, this mother had the complication of a bad back. When her youngster would dash away from her, as two and two-and-a-half-year-olds will, she was physically as well as emotionally unable to manage him. Her near panic on such occasions was upsetting to the boy, yet he seemed impelled to make her chase after him time and again.

"I suppose this is what it is like if you have a brother," this mother would exclaim in exasperation.

The way she phrased her helplessness pointed to the fact that without being aware of it, she had feared having a brother when she was a girl.

FEELINGS ABOUT ONESELF AFFECT FEELINGS ABOUT ONE'S ELDEST

A couple who are getting along reasonably well together much of the time, who are able to give each other some affection, some companionship, and some sexual fulfillment, will probably be able to give their first baby the love he needs. From that love a baby develops a sense of basic trust in his parents and gradually confidence in himself and in his surroundings.

A woman who is disappointed in her husband may concentrate too much hovering attention on her first baby. A man who feels that his marriage is standing in the way of his career or that his wife's extravagance or social ambition or restlessness is putting a heavy burden on him may not have a warm welcome for his eldest. Because of worries only indirectly connected with the baby, a man may not take kindly to fatherhood or a woman to motherhood.

Whether a father is finding satisfaction in his work, whether a mother likes keeping house, whether they both have some refreshing recreation and feel that they are accepted, contributing members of their community affects their attitude toward their first-born. How they feel about their own parents and in-laws are prominent pieces in the intricate patchwork pattern of feelings about their first child. What they like or dislike in themselves influences how they respond to a child's behavior, too. The baby who is truly wanted tends to have a more favorable setting for his development than one whose arrival was planned merely because his parents decided that having a baby was the thing to do.

Some adverse conditions prevail at times for a day or a week in almost every family. Nobody continuously gives his best to a baby or to anyone else. Transient resentments and strains rarely leave the scars some parents fear they may. Underlying attitudes that persist, however—responses that are repeated over and over again—leave their imprint on personality.

"OUR LIFE'S STAR HATH ELSEWHERE HAD ITS SETTING"

In the new family which comes into being when the first baby arrives, many forces combine to shape the parents' feelings about themselves, the newcomer, and each other. Shadows from the past stand beside a mother and father as they look at their infant in his crib. They themselves as youngsters, the eldest in their own families, even the brother or sister they never had will contribute indirectly to their attitudes toward this new personality. These shadows, plus their own ideals and aspirations and uncertainties, will be making an impression on their child day by day through the years.

How strongly these influences will be felt depends on whether they are reinforced or mitigated by other external circumstances. These emotional hand-me-downs from a parent's own youth cannot be obliterated. But understanding their source and their universality makes you better able to cope with them. Such understanding can release an individual to work toward a solution of difficulties, for understanding used wisely is a spur to action, not an excuse for doing nothing when action is in order.

Into each situation we bring much that is useful from our past, as well as a few notions and attitudes that get in our way. Only as we bring from our childhood homes those customs, standards, and ways of living together which we value, can the traditions our society cherishes be handed on and modified in each new family. The eldest is frequently the one who carries on this tradition.

CHAPTER III

While the Eldest Is the Only One

The eldest in the family has the unique experience of at first having his parents for himself, with no rivals of his own generation, and then finding he must share them. He is somewhat like Dr. Doolittle's Pushmi-pullyu, that remarkable animal who had a head at both ends of his body and wanted to go forward and backward at the same time.

To be without brothers and sisters throughout childhood is generally reckoned a misfortune, but to be an only child for a few years can be a great stroke of luck. From it the first child may reap many benefits, but there are also difficulties to be surmounted in being an only child for even a short time.

Many children today have a brother or sister before they are able to walk alone, but having been an only child will still have made a lasting impression. Being the first born does not determine what kind of person a child will become or what his lot will be. A great number of strengths and weaknesses are inherent in the situation. There are those who say, "I was the oldest and I was top dog." Others insist, "It's tough having a bunch of little ones trailing after you whatever you do." Many persons will tell you of the alternating benefits and deprivations they have felt because of being eldest, but it is a rare individual who has no feeling one way or another about it.

Which of the potential assets and liabilities will be highlighted and which remain in the shadow depends on the interaction of a child's own constitution with his surroundings and with the personalities of those who are important to him as he is growing up.

WHAT DOES IT MEAN TO BE KING FOR A DAY?

While he is the only child, a boy or girl is likely to feel particularly close to his parents. To them, their first baby seems almost a miracle. It is not surprising that he absorbs the feeling of being special. If this highly agreeable arrangement of being one of a threesome with his parents continues for several years, it appears to the child to be the normal state of affairs.

This is a state which a first child may, without realizing it, always hope to duplicate after the arrival of another baby. Some eldests all through life continue to look for a relationship in which they can be the one and only. Sadly enough, the more such persons demand complete possession of a parent in their childhood, or of friend or spouse in adulthood, the more they are likely to be disappointed.

A temporarily only child forms a different picture of himself and his parents than his younger brothers and sisters will have of themselves. Being the sole recipient of his mother's attention for a year or two may give him an extra degree of self-esteem for life. Yet his dethronement when another baby arrives will be more of a shock than a second or third child will suffer under similar circumstances. These inner pulls and tensions play a part in shaping the personality of the eldest.

IT'S A STELLAR ROLE

Everything about the first child is exciting to his parents. No matter how familiar a man or woman may be with the ways of babies, a baby of one's own is different. That one is more appealing, more attractive, and certainly brighter than any other, as even the most impartial parents will attest.

As the baby grows, each new accomplishment is a great event. Mothers and fathers wonder how outsiders can be so calloused to the marvels of his walking, talking, and before long riding a tricycle and bringing in the morning newspaper without being told to do so.

Parents are likely to have more time and perhaps more inclination to talk at length to the eldest, even before he can understand their words. They sing to him, tell him stories, and take him around with them. If he continues to be the only one for several years, his questions are probably answered more fully and with more interest than will be the case when several children claim parental attention simultaneously. The dawn of an intellectual sunrise is sweeter and more awe-inspiring the first time than the second, third, or fourth time a mother is asked those searching questions about why it rains, or why Mary Jane's father doesn't work as hard as daddy, but has two cars.

Because the eldest is more in the company of adults he is likely to talk earlier, and with a richer vocabulary. He is prodded toward intellectual attainments, and up to a point may respond to the prodding. The popular notion that because younger children learn from the oldest and from one another they are more advanced intellectually in their early years has not held up in the findings of a recent study. This study of six- and seven-year-olds indicated that oldest boys are frequently ahead of oldest girls in the development of some mental abilities. One suggested explanation is that a boy is likely to have more attention from his mother than a girl does if she is the eldest.

ADULTS ARE HIS PACE SETTERS

An eldest child has only adults for his models in his early years. For that reason only and oldest children tend to be more serious. Many of them are considered bookworms and goody-goodies by their contemporaries and little old men or perfect ladies by adults. An only or eldest child has not learned that human beings have many years to grow and that they are not expected to equal the achievements of their parents. A first-born measures himself against his parents even when the standards they set for him are not exacting. For this reason, some eldest children look with mistrust all their lives on the crude beginnings of an enterprise.

One small boy who repeatedly expressed the wish for an older brother was voicing this dilemma. "If I only had a big brother I'd know what to do," he would say in a worried voice. His father, not realizing that exactly here was the rub, would suggest that he might substitute for a big brother.

"You're all right for a Daddy, but you're an old man. If I had big brothers the way Joey has, they'd show me how to whistle through my fingers and how to turn cartwheels."

The first child in the family, in trying to be adult beyond his years, may develop a burdensome conscience. This accounts for his primness and also gives rise to a nice problem for parents and teachers. A good, working conscience makes for a responsible individual and is to be encouraged. Yet in some eldest children it works overtime. No adult would add to a youngster's worries by making him feel his conscientiousness is displeasing, but over-emphasizing that excellent quality is unwise. The boy or girl who is too anxious about standing well with adults can be given the feeling that everyone becomes involved in mischief, makes mistakes, or forgets once in a while, and that occasional failures make him no less loved. Too much exhortation to be a big boy or behave like mother's big helper is to be avoided with a child who has a sensitive conscience, especially when the second baby appears on the scene.

Can this picture of many eldest children, as sober and conscientious in comparison with the others in the family, be reconciled with the fact that the proportion of eldest children who are brought to child guidance clinics is greater than the proportion in the general population? The explanation may well be that parents are more concerned over the behavior of the eldest because of their own inexperience and therefore seek help with him more readily. Flagrant misbehavior is not the only reason for bringing a child to a guidance clinic.

THE OLDEST ALLIES HIMSELF WITH ADULTS

An eldest many times thinks of himself as allied to the adults around him, rather than to the children. In *The Fountain Over-*

flows, Rebecca West (N.Y., Viking, 1956) sums up the delicate position of an oldest daughter. The two younger girls in the novel, knowing their mother is troubled, are attempting to offer a solution for her distress. The youngest who tells the story, says of Cordelia, the eldest sister:

"Cordelia shook her head at us and frowned and hushed us, as well as kicking us under the table. It was like Cordelia to use both grown-up and childish means of expressing disapprobation, she was always on both sides if she could be."

Another method of trying to be on both sides is prevalent in one of the Polynesian groups. There an oldest child will often reinforce the command of a parent or grandparent by calling out to the younger ones, "Mind mother now," or "Mind grandfather." Our own oldest children, too, do much the same thing with more than a trace of smugness in the admonition. Back of this echo of the command is the feeling, "I am good. I know what one must do."

The fact that eldest children so often aspire to be trained nurses, teachers, and policemen is attributed by some investigators to their early feeling of being responsible caretakers.

Taking on the feeling of the older generation has its gratifying side, too. From talks with a number of adolescent oldest girls, statements like these came out repeatedly:

"You sort of bring your parents up when you're the oldest. I mean, they have to practice on you and it makes you closer."

"Because I'm the oldest, my mother treats me more as if I were an adult."

"Mother likes us all, but she can talk to me differently. We've been more like sisters."

"Mother and I like to do the same things and we think the same things are funny."

"I like being the oldest because I get to do things with my mother more than the little ones do."

GUARANTEED TO BE FRESH AND NOT SHOPWORN

An only child will seldom hear the cry, "You'll have to wait," or "It isn't your turn," or "You're taking more than your share," when he wants an extra good-night story, asks to sit in the front seat of the family automobile right next to his father, or grabs the biggest cookie on the plate. Even if his wishes are denied, at least nobody else gets what he was trying to have. On a comparative basis, needs and requests of the eldest are met more promptly and fully than demands will be when parental attention and family resources must be divided between two, three, or five children.

Attainments of the eldest are greeted with a zest that will not be repeated for the later arrivals in the family. Birthday parties and school plays, the production of clumsy but lovingly made gifts, and compositions played haltingly on the piano by the first child are great events for parents. As one mother phrased it, "The smaller boys never had any toys that their oldest brother hadn't put some dents in and there were a few dents in papa and mama by the time the second and third and fourth ones came along, too."

Another mother, when asked whether she felt there was a marked difference between her handling of her first daughter and the younger ones, answered, "It's been hand-me-downs all along the line for the younger ones, but of course we're more relaxed with them, and we never were all thumbs when they were babies, either."

IT'S A DRESS REHEARSAL

"We're more relaxed with the younger ones" tells the story of the disadvantages which may fall to the lot of the eldest. With a first baby parents may see danger signs where none exist. Almost inevitably they lack a sense of perspective. The feeling that "it's happened before and it will happen again" is the essence of a healthy sense of proportion. That usually comes to those who have watched some of the ups and downs of childhood from the vantage point of a parent.

Although both a mother and father may be unaccustomed to babies, one may have had a background to draw upon to reassure both of them. A father, who as a farmer had spent most of his life around calves and lambs, had a keen eye for the difference between a healthy young animal and one that was on the droopy side. When his city-bred wife would be anxious because their baby was restless or would not eat, he would tell her, "If this were a lamb, I'd say all signs point to its being all right and the signs are probably the same with babies. I'll bet if you stop fussing over her, she'll be fine." His gentle touch and his quiet, easy voice were as soothing to his little daughter as to her tense and worried mother. A man who can comfort his wife when she is upset over the first baby is being the best kind of father.

Some young mothers and fathers in their eagerness to be good parents may try out every idea they encounter. It is helpful to remember that a youngster need not be a composite picture of the desirable qualities of every child in the neighborhood, nor is a parent required to be perfect. If parents can let their child, from babyhood on, be himself, he will undoubtedly have his full share of lovable and useful traits.

Some parents have definite ideas of what kind of person they want their child to be and set standards that are too high for him, not just when he is a baby but throughout childhood. They expect too much, too soon, until they learn to put more trust in the forces of development.

The specter of the spoiled child haunts many young parents. Lest their first child commit those sins which might place him in that category, they are unduly severe. Later they discover that extreme strictness and continually denying a child what he wants, which they once thought prevented spoiling, may make a youngster more demanding. The two- or three-year-old who knows he will usually get what he needs, whether it is a kiss or a cracker, who has had many satisfactions, can more easily accept reasonable restriction without too much protest.

In an effort to be casual, some parents elect to run their lives with a complete lack of organization until they discover that some routines, however flexible, can still preserve the atmosphere of relaxation they find congenial. Like landmarks and fences on the open prairie, such routines keep a mother from losing a sense of direction completely as she goes about the day's business.

Most first babies probably get a shade too much or a shade less organization than would be ideal for them without being any the worse for it. Babies are tough. Small children have a resiliency that should not be underestimated.

WHEN THE ACTORS ARE UNPREPARED

Since the eldest is in a sense the dress rehearsal for his parents' performance in raising a family, it is not surprising that they may be inadequately prepared for the parts they are to play. Some parents have not acquired that knack of getting on together which our grandparents described as trotting smoothly in double harness. They have not worked out their own tensions sufficiently to meet the further demands parenthood makes. If they are not always ready consciously or unconsciously to settle down to the tasks and restrictions a baby imposes, it may be because they are still too romantically absorbed in each other. Particularly in the United States where the cult of the young girl holds sway, a woman in her early twenties may approach motherhood with a twinge of regret.

That was the feeling of Connie Lang, who had been a popular beauty in college. She had a secret fear that once she was a mother she would lose her figure and her charm. She regarded her friends who had become mothers as dowdy in appearance and stodgy in conversation. Her all-star football husband, too, believed that becoming a father might land him in the thinning-hair, thickening-waist-line class.

Fortunately, the Lang's baby girl was blessed with doting grandparents. Their affectionate warmth filled in some of the gaps until her parents were convinced that mothering and fathering were, if not quite as entertaining, still as important as going to a football game or square dancing.

The Langs gradually discovered that being a mother and father did not plunge them headlong into middle age. Being quite willing to do what everybody else was doing, no matter what that might be, they were able to fit into the pattern of parenthood their friends were following.

Like many young parents who are immature when their first child is born, the Langs were able to grow. Many young parents do attain the stamina they need to raise a family through training on the job.

Couples like the Langs cannot be dismissed as merely shallow and selfish. If they are not ready to give their first baby all he needs emotionally, it may not be due entirely to their personal shortcomings. When every movie, every advertisement, and the atmosphere of the homes in which they grew up have put the accent on youth, how can maturity and all it entails be attractive?

From another viewpoint, the youthfulness of parents when their first child is born is an advantage. Youth is proverbially more energetic, more elastic, less muscle-bound in every way. Those who can sit on the floor for an hour without getting stiff in the joints can probably enjoy playing with a small child and are better able to see life from a child's point of view in every way. Looking back on the first years of parenthood, one mother voices a general feeling, "When we were in our twenties things were rough for us, but we felt there were plenty of years ahead when they'd be better. When you're older you just haven't so much bounce. You get scared that you're caught in a trap."

WHEN PARENTHOOD COMES LATER IN LIFE

Young people may be more resilient in the face of serious troubles, but on the other hand those who are older have a better perspective on the petty restrictions and inconveniences of being a parent.

What is lost in companionability, and the greater ability to get down to a child's level, is gained by being less competitive if the first child is born later in his parent's life. This holds true particularly in the case of mothers and daughters. A mother whose girl reached the stage of walking into the mother's sweaters and skirts and walking off with her lipstick and perfume when the mother was in her mid-forties says, "If my daughter had turned into a young lady when I was 36 and still being told I looked 26—and believing I did—I think I'd have been a little annoyed at her being prettier and smarter looking than I. Now I just relax and am proud of her."

On the credit side of the ledger in having children later in life is also the mellowness and experience of the older man or woman. Greater understanding and better judgment are frequently the result of having discovered one's own capabilities and limitations. The first baby who is born to parents deep in their thirties or in their forties may be welcomed even more enthusiastically than the child of younger parents.

Still, sheer physical energy is usually less abundant and adaptability tends to grow less with the years. By the time these late-arriving eldests get to be ten—and a mother is forty-five and a father approaching fifty—the noise, the disorder, the speech, and manners of a fifth-grader may be far more taxing than they would have been a decade earlier. Then parents may look at their contemporaries whose children are in high school or college with some envy. Yet when those same children of their friends are grown and married, the older couple will still have young people at home.

PARENTS' ANGER OR FEARS MAY SHORT-CHANGE THE ELDEST

That the eldest, especially during the years he is the only child, is likely to bear the brunt of his mother's and father's inner conflicts to a greater extent than the younger children do is a point on which authorities seem to be agreed. Neither Avis nor Bill McKinstrey, had moved far away from their own parents either geographically or emotionally. The young couple had settled in the same medium-sized town where both sets of parents lived. Though neither Bill nor Avis put the feeling into words, both were struggling to stand on their own feet and put an end to their childish dependence on their own parents. As a result both of them bristled when it seemed as if mother, father, mother-in-law or father-in-law were giving them advice or interfering.

A friendly phone call from his mother would be followed by an outburst from Bill. If his father dropped in with an innocent question about plans for next Sunday, the young man would be in a bad temper for the rest of the evening. Avis was sure to have a headache if she had spent the afternoon with her mother.

When their baby came, Bill and Avis were determined to bring her up their way with no assistance or intervention from the grandparents. Because the young couple were still struggling to work out their relationship to their own parents, their daughter had a more meager life during her first years than she might otherwise have had. Grandparents would have tripled the number of people whom she trusted. Being at ease in her grandparents' homes would have helped overcome an inclination to cling to her mother and back away from anything new.

When a second child was born, expediency overcame false pride. Avis found that letting her daughter spend some time with each of the grandmothers made things simpler at home. Since Avis and Bill had grown somewhat more sure of themselves and less afraid of being treated like children, Avis' anxiety about the grandmothers' spoiling the girl or trying to run the McKinstrey household by remote control decreased too.

Sometimes parents have groundless fears or prejudices which influence the way they bring up their first child, but do not so much effect children who come later. A mother who is terrified of water may refuse to let her oldest learn to swim. Yet when younger children clamor for swimming lessons, she may be able to let them learn and let the eldest go swimming as well, although she has slight peace of mind while they are in the water. Parents who are concerned lest their first child come under the supposed bad influence of children from different backgrounds often are able to be far more tolerant of the companions of their younger children.

THE USES OF ADVERSITY

Because of the hurdles he has been forced to surmount, an eldest may become a person of unusual sensitivity, able to respond to and identify with the troubles of his fellow man to a greater degree than could one for whom life had gone more smoothly.

While nonconformity is not in itself a goal, when it takes the shape of originality, independence, and the ability to defend one's convictions it is frequently a healthy manifestation. It is more constructive to help such a child find serviceable ways to use his special qualities than to insist he fit into the conventional mould. He cannot be permitted to be a disturbing force at home or in a group, yet he can be guided so that his abilities are not stifled.

Katherine in the *Taming of the Shrew* was such a fiery eldest. For all her bad temper she was a more vibrant, interesting personality than the saccharine, younger Bianca. Some of Kate's disagreeableness may have been the result of competing with the highly concentrated sweetness of the favored younger girl. Some of it may have been forcefulness gone sour because no means of draining off surplus energy and high spirits had been provided. A Katherine whose vigor had been channeled and reduced—and not necessarily by the techniques of Petruchio—would still have been far more of a person than her docile sister. She would have been a happier, more contributing individual too than if she had been merely cowed in childhood.

Parents may be comforted to know, that among those who attain emminence there are a high proportion of eldests, as a number of studies have demonstrated.

ONLY NEED NOT EQUAL LONELY

Sociability ranks high as one of the goals adults hold for children. Sociability is the best balance wheel for too much solicitous protection. The classic disadvantage of being an only child is lack of practice in standing up for one's own rights and sharing with other children. When the period of being an only child lasts a year, or a year and a half, this drawback has slight chance to appear. Careful planning can counterbalance the lack for those who remain only children for several years.

Only children differ widely in the degree of friendliness or shyness, selfishness or generosity, they may show in their early years. Small boys and girls are rarely willing sharers no matter how many there may be in the family. Indeed, if what he shares he loses, the youngster with several brothers and sisters may hang on more tenaciously to his toys than one whose experiences have been less bitter. Generosity comes more readily at any age if you have not found it too costly.

There is often a wide gulf between being eager for companionship and knowing how to enjoy it. The only child may be less adept at getting along with children than the one who has been exposed to the pulling and hauling, backing and filling, grabbing and defending which is the hourly portion of those who grow up together under the same roof.

Companionship has different meanings at different ages. At eighteen months, two youngsters in the same room may seem oblivious of each others' company except when one pokes or pushes the other. At this age, infants are not ready to play with or be left alone with others of similar age. Nevertheless, just watching a creature like himself is a useful experience for an infant. The pinching and shoving is merely sensible curiosity as to whether this person is alive or stuffed, whether he will laugh or cry, whether he is able to get around under his own steam.

A few months or a year later, two or three youngsters may play alongside of one another. They enjoy being in one another's company for short periods, but there is little joint activity—a fact which distresses mothers who have taken considerable trouble to bring the children together. The toddlers get more out of these contacts than one might imagine and being near one another does foster sociability in boys and girls who have no brothers and sisters.

Three-year-olds, and to a greater extent four-year-olds, are usually happy for at least part of the day playing around the neighborhood. They are still not equal to really cooperative ventures, but anyone old enough to be trusted as far as the corner can merge into or fade out of whatever may be afoot at will. A youngster may return home several times in the course of a morning insisting he won't play with those girls anymore," only to sally forth half an hour later and rejoin the group down the block.

Four-year-olds begin to have special friends and to discriminate as to whom they like and dislike. Two or four do better playing together than three, for one is sure to be left out while the others whisper secrets. An adult who waits fifteen minutes before preaching democracy and friendliness, or deciding that the one who is excluded does not know how to play, may find a realignment of alliances taking place.

Play groups and nursery schools make a contribution to the threes and fours who are only children. Interestingly enough, it is the opposite value from what a child with a younger brother or sister or two gains. The only child profits by companionship, while the one who has a surfeit of that at home may find relative peace. In nursery school, children can play together without the demands of the guest-host relationship. The short period away from their mothers is educational, too. Poise and self-reliance are fostered as children discover that it is possible to get along happily both at home and away from home. Most nursery schools ease a new member of the group in gradually with mothers staying around as long as seems necessary during the first few weeks. A good nursery school can bring out the innate capacity for friendliness. (The question of the eldest in nursery groups is discussed in detail in Chapter VII.)

Dorothy Canfield Fisher, many years ago, gave a picture in *Understood Betsy* (N.Y., Grosset & Dunlap, 1917) of what happens when a child is hovered over incessantly.

At a quarter of nine every week-day morning Aunt Frances dropped whatever else she was doing, took Elizabeth Ann's little, thin, white hand protectingly in hers, and led her to the big, brick school building. . . . You can imagine perhaps, the noise there was on the playground just before school! Elizabeth Ann shrank from it with all her soul, and clung more tightly than ever to Aunt Frances' hand. . . . Oh, how glad she was that she had Aunt Frances there to take care of her. Aunt Frances took her safely through the ordeal of the playground. . . . and pigeonholed her carefully in her own schoolroom. . . . Then at noon Aunt Frances was waiting. . . . and in the afternoon the same thing happened over again. Aunt Frances believed in sympathizing with a child's life, so she always asked about every little thing. . . . Sometimes in telling over some very dreadful failure or disappointment, Elizabeth Ann would get so wrought up that she would cry. This always brought the ready tears to Aunt Frances' kind eyes. . . . The days when they had cried they could neither of them eat much luncheon.

The change from being only to being eldest is not made without some pangs. If the possible advantages of being an only one have been realized, and the disadvantages reduced, healthy personality probably has had a sound foundation. If forces of development have been understood and fostered, rewards will be likely to balance difficulties for the boy or girl who takes on the proud position of the eldest in the family.

CHAPTER IV

The Next Arrival

When the second baby is on the way, a mother is quite a different person from what she was while she awaited her first one. She is more poised and knowledgeable. Both parents are probably better able to give the new baby the mothering and the fathering he will need. They will do much the same things in caring for the new baby as they did for their first-born, but there will be a subtle, yet definite change in how they feel about what they do.

WHAT DOES NEW BABY MEAN TO THE OLDER ONE?

When the first-born realizes that the constant association of the new baby and his own indispensable mother is to be a permanent affair, he faces distressing questions. These unworded but deeply felt perplexities add up to, "What does this interloper do to my place with mother and father?"

Parents might as well be prepared for both the older one's affection and his anger. Both pride and resentment toward the baby and also toward his mother for bringing such complications into his life will undoubtedly appear. The opposing feelings which exist side by side in human beings affect every relationship. This is one reason why the roots of the older child's jealousy go deep, but the roots of his affection are equally far reaching. The capacity for loving the baby is present even though the elder's actions may belie it. A youngster would like to possess his parents completely and exclusively. To a small child, affection is like a cake. Every time someone else gets a piece, he imagines that much less remains for him.

45

A new baby in the family has different meanings to children of different ages. Two-and-a-half and three-year-olds will talk about wanting a baby. Four- and five-year-olds wish for a brother or sister both for companionship and because other boys and girls have one or more. The child who longs for a brother or sister with whom he can play does not realize that an addition to the family will necessitate his sharing his parents.

Each age responds to the real event in its own way, and each age needs a special kind of supporting affection. No child will show all the kinds of behavior described here. For the two- to five-year-old, the full import, pleasant and unpleasant, of having a brother or sister generally does not come with the announcement of the future event. Even the arrival may be taken in stride. Its real meaning may become apparent only when the younger one is able to get around under his own power and seems to constitute a menace to the elder.

While the baby stays in his crib, the older child is more likely to be angry with his mother for what seems to be her desertion. The older one's troubled feelings may also be due to inner conflicts not directly connected with the baby. These are often touched off or brought to the surface by the presence of the newcomer. The resulting explosion is like the conflagration that takes place when oil-soaked rags ignite because they are near an intense heat.

DON'T BE AFRAID OF STRONG FEELINGS

The feelings of the first-born confronted with the fact that another baby is coming have often been compared to the feelings a wife would have if her husband told her, "I love you so much I think it would be twice as nice to have two wives." Both situations entail the indignity and discomfort of having only a half interest in the person who is vital to your well-being. Both would raise the question, "What is wrong with me that I am not sufficient?" "What have I done to deserve this?"

Of course, a child does not feel constantly distressed, but he has many low moments before he discovers that a brother or sister does not spell "no more mother," and that it brings satisfactions of its own.

Parents frequently complain, "We've done all the things the books said, and our daughter is still jealous." The essential point which those who write the books make, and which is too often overlooked, is that while parents cannot hope to give displacment a pleasing flavor, they can take away some of the bitter taste so that the new regime will be at least palatable to the older child some of the time. Just because parents have not worked a miracle does not mean that they have wasted their time.

An initial step in helping the first-born may be some rearrangement of a parent's own values. There is a widespread feeling that if you save the surface, you save all. As long as strong feelings do not rear their ugly heads success seems to have crowned the effort.

Certain authors and copywriters proclaim that serenity is wonderful and available to all. These claims have made us feel that if our children are not always merry, that if we do not make a jolly celebration out of every occasion, we are falling short. We are almost as grim about having fun these days as were our Puritan forebears about avoiding the agreeable. Neither extreme makes sense. The ability to be both sad and glad as circumstances warrant is the beginning of wisdom and of a healthy personality.

As for strong feelings, they can show up in a variety of behavior. The boy or girl who is coming to terms with the problem of a new brother or sister is not necessarily the one who is not showing signs of resentment. Open jealousy in and of itself is not a goal, yet parents may have accomplished a great deal in making it possible for a child to express his feelings about the baby.

It would be a mistake, however, to conclude that *only* those children who show their resentment plainly are in a state of emotional well-being. Take into consideration, everything a child is doing rather than look at isolated incidents before judging how he is responding to the new state of affairs.

BREAKING THE NEWS

The custom has been to lay great emphasis on what is said or done and when it is said or done in preparing the eldest for the next arrival. Preparation in the best sense is less a matter of techniques used three weeks or three months before the baby comes and more a matter of the experiences and relationships that a youngster has had all along the way.

The phrases mothers and fathers will use in making the announcement have so often been explained that they do not need repetition here. As long as no one misrepresents the situation, and parents do not put themselves in a position where the eldest can say, "Why did you fool me?," they are probably on the right track.

The timing of the announcement will depend somewhat on convenience. If a mother's appearance has altered early in her pregnancy, there may be direct questions from an observant youngster. Other circumstances might make a relatively early conversation about the arrival simpler for everyone. If coming events do not cast too long a shadow before them, the three- or four- or five-year-old will probably follow the lead of the adults around him and not be unduly absorbed with the idea of the new baby. Talking too much, too early, and too often about the brother- or sister-to-be can be disturbing to a young child for whom long waits are unbearable. Still, when parents break the news is less vital than how they break it. A more detailed discussion of how questions of the "where is the baby now?" type may be answered is to be found in *Brothers and Sisters*.[1]

Try as an adult may, not to glorify the newborn, a child may get a false impression of how the baby will look and what he will be able to do. Since seeing is believing, a visit to a friend who has obligingly had a baby recently may serve to scale down to size a small child's image of a newborn.

If a mother plans to nurse the baby, it will be especially helpful if the older one sees another mother nursing hers. If he realizes that breast feeding is not a unique whim of his own mother but a well-established custom, it may not seem to him that his brother or sister is enjoying a rare privilege which he is denied.

A certain amount of repetition gives a young child the opportunity to make an idea his own. Books about new babies and their families are useful as a supplement or if need be as a substitute for a personal acquaintance with a newborn. You may find these

[1] Edith G. Neisser, Harper & Brothers, 1951.

picture books good to read to the three, four, five- or six-year-old both before and after the baby is in the house: Nancy Langstaff and Susanne Szasz, *A Tiny Baby For You*, (N.Y., Scribners, 1955); Norma Simon, *Baby House*, (Phila., Lippincott, 1955); Ruth and Harold, Shane, *The New Baby*, (N.Y., Simon & Schuster, 1948).

ONE CHANGE AT A TIME

The change in his relationship to his parents is enough for a youngster to assimilate when he makes the actual transition from only to elder child. The tangible changes that necessarily accompany the enlarging of the family are more easily accepted if they do not all occur at once. If new arrangements are concluded well before the second baby arrives, so that the first child has become accustomed to them before he must become accustomed to the baby itself, he will probably find them less upsetting.

He can be introduced to a new bed, or a switch in rooms a month or two in advance of the baby's birth. If for practical reasons, certain alterations in routines or equipment cannot be made ahead of time, it is usually possible to plan so that a child is not required to adjust to one strange procedure before another has become familiar. Experience has proved new arrangements are more readily accepted if they are explained a few days before they occur. Surprises all too often turn out to be shocks and give a child the feeling that the ground is being cut away from under him.

If a boy or girl is to attend nursery school, he will as a rule accept the new situation with a better grace if he is started in the group six weeks or two months before the baby arrives rather than immediately afterward. The baby drives a wedge between the elder one and his mother at best. Adding the separation nursery school entails may make the the older one feel he has been thrust to the rim of outer space.

Arrangements for the older child, that help him accept the arrival of the baby when a mother goes to the hospital and when she returns are also described in *Brothers and Sisters*.

NOW THAT THE BABY IS HERE

The way the first-born will respond to the presence of the new brother or sister will depend upon his phase of development, his relationship to his parents, and on all the other things that have happened and are happening to him. The older child is confronted not simply with a new baby. He must cope with a complicated web of new baby plus learning to talk, or new baby plus new house plus grandfather having died recently, or new baby plus starting school plus a painful illness last month. This web is one reason why the best preparations do not always produce the hoped-for results.

The more helpless a child is, the more his mother represents a life-line to everything he wants and needs. In his delightful autobiography, *Over the Bridge* (N.Y., Dutton, 1956), Richard Church expresses what a mother stands for. He is speaking of a child of seven, but in even greater degree this holds true for a younger one.

My universe was still centered in my mother's fragrant person: her lap, her caress, her hair and eyes so curiously the same nut brown color, warm and glowing. The garments she took off—the apron, the dropped handkerchief—shone for awhile with her light. . . . She and these detachable attributes were like the sun and his flakes of fire. The further I got from her, the colder and darker fell my living days and nights. And the fall was rapid: so small was my own supply of vitality, the confidence of flesh and bone.

If a youngster must make room for a junior member of the family before he is two, he cannot be expected to relinquish too speedily those comforts granted to babies. He is still an infant himself in most respects.

His feelings range from a vague sense that something has changed to near panic when he sees his mother giving the newcomer the kind of attention he believes is due him alone. Yet showing how angry he is might be too dangerous. It might drive her away altogether.

"I WANT TO BE A BABY, TOO"

Most of the time a child does his best to please his parents. Much of the trouble he gets into results from his misinterpretation of what they prize. A small child's notions of cause and effect are thoroughly confused. When he sees the baby getting the attention he wants he concludes without being able to put his feeling into words, "The baby is helpless. They love the baby. I will be helpless and they will love me too." Such feelings have come to light as small children have been studied.

Many three- and four-year-olds go back to babyish ways. "You do these things for the baby because you love him. Prove you love me by giving me the same comforts" is another aspect of the feeling back of this behavior.

The three- and four- and even five-year-old envies the baby's license to do those things and obtain those services he has himself only recently and with struggle renounced. This backsliding is not due entirely to jealousy. In a curious way, admiration and fondness for the baby impel the older one to imitate its behavior and identify himself with the newcomer.

The collapse of the three-, four- or five-year old's independence is even more aggravating to parents than the backsliding of the one-and-a-half- or two-year-old. Yet a parent's task with the former is easier for he can be approached in words which would be ineffective with a younger child. "I'll help you (or give you a bottle or change your pants) now, but soon I know you'll want to do it the way big girls and boys do. You'll be proud of yourself when you can do it the grown-up way." Here is a promise that growing up is worth the effort, an acknowledgement that backsliding is temporary, and proof his mother loves him enough to give him as much as she is giving the baby. As a rule, cheerfully permitting a slight retreat makes it easier to take a firm stand if a complete rout seems imminent.

Parents may need to call a halt on total backsliding, but if a degree of it, or of one kind of babyishness seems to ease the strain, it can be allowed. At the same time it is well to point out one's confidence in a child's ability to take up a "better way" soon again.

Sometimes a young child not much more than an infant himself will seem oblivious to the baby's existence. He raises no objections. He never asks the classic question, "When will we send the baby back?" even though he has the facility with words to frame it. In an effort to let sleeping dogs lie, or perhaps to show the elder he is preferred, a mother and father may be tempted to pretend to ignore the baby. This attitude can lead parents into a trap.

Instead of insisting whenever an old order changes that the status quo is the only blessed state, we would do better to let our children feel from their earliest days, "Here is something new. It may be hard to become accustomed to it, but it may prove to be something good." If we have taken that stand all along, unfamiliarity will be less likely to spell disaster.

Those who have worked with small children have discovered that they sense the falseness in any pretense that having a baby in the house makes no difference. A child may himself at times deny that the baby exists, but if the grown-ups pretend the same, he is likely to be upset. Children feel more secure when their parents are firmly anchored in the real world.

Just as parents should be honest when they talk about the baby before its birth, so they will come off better if they are honest about their feelings after it has joined the family circle. Mothers and fathers love each of their children. The important lesson for the eldest to grasp, in so far as he is able to, is that mothers and fathers have enough love for more than one child.

"Once you were a baby and we did these things for you. Now you are bigger and we do other things together and you can do so much more," is a sounder tactic.

Parents are frequently advised not to cuddle the baby in the presence of the older child. In following this sound advice they do not need to deny their first child the chance to express his affection. They can foster his kindlier feelings toward a brother or sister by letting him touch and play with the baby. Latent affection is more likely to flourish as a small child finds that babies can be lovable and enjoyable. If hugs are so vigorous as to arouse the suspicion that they are not prompted by love, they should be supervised gently.

WHEN FEEDING TIME IS A TENSION POINT

Since food spells love, the baby's feedings are likely to be the hardest times in the day for the one- or two- or three- or four-year-old, and feeding comes often in a new baby's life. Mothers can probably arrange matters so that the first meeting between the two children does not occur while the baby is being fed, especially if the baby is being nursed. It will hardly be possible to keep the older one out of the way at feeding times beyond that, if a mother is caring for two or more. To do so would only multiply complications. Many youngsters can take the mealtime closeness of mother and baby more readily if they have a cracker to nibble or a glass of fruit juice to sip. Many seize this moment to show off or engage in some bit of deviltry.

One mother turned this demand for attention to good account. As soon as she had settled herself in a chair to feed the baby, her two-year-old began to show off. His proudest accomplishment was to fall to the floor putting his hands out in front of him just in time to land in a push-up position. It was a praiseworthy feat requiring no small amount of coordination. The mother would call the two-year-old when the baby was to be fed, and encourage him to repeat his act for her entertainment. This made him feel important and kept him where she could watch him.

If parents are able to see either the mischief or the more direct bid for the limelight as an immature attempt at a solution to a problem rather than as sheer malice, they can deal with it more effectively. The goal is not a child who is self-effacing, but a child who obtains the attention he wants, and needs, without becoming destructive. A youngster who goes through the tricks in his repertoire which have won admiration on other occasions is solving his problem in a sensible way on his own level.

Boys and girls who feel they are playing second fiddle can be encouraged to find acceptable ways to bid for a solo part. Sometimes they can be steered into an activity like putting a record on their record-player to entertain a mother while she is feeding the baby. A three- or four-year-old can bring a well-loved book and tell about the pictures. Helping by holding the bottle may tide a youngster over a bad spot. Of course the excellent device of having a girl feed her doll while her mother does the same for the baby is not to be overlooked.

"BOYS ARE BOYS AND GIRLS STAY GIRLS"

The boy who is three or four or five or six years old looks at his baby sister in her bath and begins to wonder whether she has lost that organ which in this phase of his development is so interesting and so important to him. After the birth of his sister, one three-year-old boy became restless and irritable. His mother realized that here was the opportunity to make a simple explanation. "Girls are made differently so they can grow up to be mommies. Everybody thinks its nice to have girls and to have boys in the house," she told him, reassuring him that no one changed from one sex to another and that both sexes were equally valued. As his fears were set at rest, he grew less irritable and easier to live with. His mother, wisely, did not try to find out why he felt his own masculinity was endangered, for she realized that a great many questions on her part might discourage her son from bringing up the subject.

A girl who has a baby brother may need the same kind of reassurance.

AIRING ANGRY FEELINGS

Angry feelings in some children are drained off in desirable ways. Stuffed animals or dolls may be the victims of treatment an older child would like to see meted out to the baby. There may be an epidemic of wrecks among the toy cars and trains. The displaced one may organize her friends in interminable games of housekeeping. One girl particularly enjoyed pretending she and her father were going away on a train leaving her mother and the baby at home with nothing to eat. This play neatly consigned to oblivion both her rivals and gave her complete possession of her father.

Another four-year-old frequently played that her dolls were sick because they had a "bad mommy" who did not take good care of them. Then she pretended to be the doctor who made them well. This gave expression to both her dislike of babies—they were made to be sick and uncomfortable—and her annoyance at her mother. Her kindlier feelings came to the fore as she posed as the doctor who made them well.

Such play can be an excellent safety valve. If parents listen carefully, it can tell them which way the wind blows. Paintings and drawings, made-up stories and songs also assist in getting rid of resentment that might, if it piled up inside, cause trouble.

Sometimes the doll play takes a gentler turn. Dolls get the tenderest care as a girl comes to feel she *is* a mother doing just what her own mother does for the baby. Such play both expresses and fosters a better acceptance of the new baby.

Some children frequently, and almost all at some time, use angry words or a direct attack on the baby. When this happens parents can let them know that their words hurt no one, and do not frighten adults. "It's all right to be mad, but I won't let you hurt the baby anymore than I would let anyone hurt you," lets a child know his mother or father is strong enough to stop him and that his rage is not as great as he feared. Along with other exaggerated and distorted ideas, he believes at times that he is far more powerful than he is—or even than he wants to be.

RESENTMENT WEARS MANY MASKS

Every human being uses certain devices, without being aware of them, to keep anger or anxiety or other unwelcome feelings from getting the best of his useful, reasonable ways of meeting the pressures of daily life. Sometimes anger goes underground. There may be great protests of affection for the baby. Preoccupation with the baby, fear lest some harm might come to it, insistence on staying near it are usually only a disguise, and a thin one at that, for a strong desire to have the rival out of the way.

In some instances these disguises continue in later life and show up in a domination of the mother who could not be possessed in childhood, as well as in a compulsion to manage the affairs of relatives, acquaintances, and subordinates. Such an individual really punishes them while he deludes himself that his only motive is self-sacrificing devotion and the welfare of others, and that he is unappreciated. In *Salt of the Earth* in *The Harsh Voice* (London, Cape, 1935), by Rebecca West, Alice Pemberton, an eldest daughter, reflects about her relationship with her mother:

Neither Madge nor Leo had done anything like so much for their mother as she had and she would have been willing to make even greater sacrifices, had they been accepted. . . . She had been quite willing to face a long engagement, simply because she hated to imagine what home would be like without her. . . . She had kept Madge and Leo from getting out of hand as fatherless children notoriously do . . . Well, all that hadn't been appreciated . . . Anyway, even if her mother had not valued her properly then, she ought to have learned to do so in the last few years. . . . Hadn't she noticed what her daughter had done for her during this visit? Alice had had put out of doors the horrible gipsyish old dressing gowns her mother loved . . . and had bought her some nice old lady dresses from quite a good shop. She had hired a car and taken her mother calling . . . and when [her mother and the Duchess] had settled down to chat as if they were two old cronies, she had been firm and just taken her home, for it does not do to presume on ones acquaintance with people like that. . . . But it had all gone for nothing.

A less malignant instance of this same tendency is displayed by the elder sister in Paddy Chayefsky's play, *In the Middle of the Night*. The elder sister on the surface is looking after her widower brother and maintaining his home for him with great concern for his welfare. Underneath her hovering attention is a strong drive to keep him in her power.

In both these instances the elder sister's domination may be surmised to stem, at least in part, from early jealousies which had appeared, perhaps unconsciously, to be too dangerous to express openly.

Some children retreat into a shell, and become extremely quiet and shy. They appear to give up any efforts to hold their own. They have not relinquished the contest for their parents' attention, but they are trying a different means of winning it. This retirement may take a sharper toll of psychological energy than open outbursts.

Sometimes a child turns his anger inward on himself. His attitude becomes, "I'm no good. No use trying. I won't be able to do it." Because such a boy or girl is less trouble than the one whose anger is on the surface and directed toward other persons, he may not get the help he needs.

Children who have another kind of temperament may become extremely active, restless, and even destructive. They are driven to do something to ease gnawing doubts about their own value which jealousy suggests. These youngsters may have tried being inconspicuous and good. When they felt they were overlooked, they resorted to more violent measures.

Usually, a combination of disguises are found to cover resentment. Contradictory feelings may appear within a short space of time. Devotion to the baby may alternate within the hour with irritation. The mood which brings exclamations of pleasure because "he's the cutest baby in the whole world" is no more lasting than the mood in which the three-year-old insisted he would "stuff the smelly old baby in the garbage."

Each child responds in his own way to stress. The breakthrough of undesirable behavior usually comes at his weakest point. Hard won, but tenuously held outposts in independence and maturity tend to be the first to fall. The two-year-old who has been slow to talk may lapse into silence. The three-year-old who has been a poor sleeper may have periods of wakefulness or become a night prowler after the baby comes. A four-year-old who has been a reluctant visitor in the homes of his playmates may refuse to go away from home for a time.

Much of the disturbing behavior that shows up in the eldest may seem to be unrelated to his feelings about his brother or sister. Fears, inability to get along with other children, refusal to eat, or almost any other signs of upset may crop out.

THE BABY IS NOT ALWAYS THE VILLAIN IN THE PIECE

Before a parent or a nursery school teacher decide that there is a deep meaning in Johnny's refusal to wear his shoes, they should be sure that the shoes are not being rejected because they are too small and uncomfortable.

The three-year-old who suffers a marked loss of appetite may be refusing to eat because in the general confusion of adjusting to new housekeeping routines her mother has not bothered much about providing tasty or varied meals. The peanut butter sandwiches formerly welcomed at lunch pall if they are served at every meal. Monotony, not jealousy, may be the root of the trouble.

BALM FOR TROUBLED SPIRITS

If obvious and common sense causes of sudden changes in a child's behavior have been ruled out and resentment seems to be at the root of it, the first step is to reassure a boy or girl that he is still important and loved. His misbehavior may be a means of getting attention but that does not mean the answer is to ignore him. His troublesome actions are symptoms of a real need for affection and encouragement. Some individuals seem to have a greater hunger for recognition than others. Every human being needs to know he is valued by other persons. Adults may have to put a stop to a child's objectionable behavior, but they can find opportunities to give him demonstrations of their affection and proof in words that they approve of him.

When parents give a child their time, they are giving him the most convincing proof of their concern for him. What is so healing to the bruised spirit of a small child as having his mother take him on her lap and tell him a story, or just visit with him? If she sits down on the floor and plays with him or takes a walk around the block, he is more sure she likes him as much as the baby.

Adults can overdo the "I know just how you feel approach," but sometimes the statement "everybody gets cross at babies and even at mothers" can go a long way toward restoring a youngster's self-respect. Adults can hold out the hope that eventually everyone gets over being angry and comes to like sisters or brothers better. It is encouraging to a child to know others have felt this way and that being angry does not cut him off from his parents' affection.

Fathers are important here for they frequently spend more time in play with the eldest. A mother's hours with a three- or four-year-old add up to greater chunks of time, but dressing, bathing, and straightening up account for a great share. A father can take the two-year-old or the four-year-old to see the trains at the station or the planes at the airport, or to watch the new house that is going up down the block, or to admire the boats on the river.

The arrival of the baby can be the moment for promoting the older one to some pleasant privileges so that being big will have concrete advantages, not merely responsibilities. A slightly later bedtime, supper with his mother and father, wider boundaries in the neighborhood, or perhaps some long-wanted piece of equipment offers proof that growing up has its desirable sides. Such promotions are also evidence that he is well thought of.

Let a small child have those things that comfort him. Favorite toys to take to bed, favorite foods at meal time may give him a lift. Even competent adults have been known to smoke a few more cigarettes or eat an extra candy bar when under pressure. Wearing a well-loved sweater even though it is almost in shreds may make a boy more contented. Putting on the dress which a mother was planning to have her daughter keep for the family Christmas dinner may be the one thing that makes life bearable for the three-year-old fashion plate.

Each child is comforted in a different way. Finding out what helps a child most can save everyone energy and heartache. A parent's encouragement and patience are invaluable to a youngster as he tries out various ways of coping with the new combination of personalities in the family.

NEW BABIES MAY ALSO BE A RELIEF

A small child's feelings about a brother or sister are made up of rivalry laced with satisfactions. Often, deep down, relief plays a part too. No matter what explanations have been made, and it is to be hoped simple and honest ones have been given, a youngster is apt to have rather confused ideas about human reproduction. An understanding of children's ideas on the subject has emerged as more has been learned in clinics and consulting rooms about children's daydreams. Many children believe that an indefinite number of babies are stored somewhere within a mother, waiting to be born. One common notion is that they are packed in like sardines in a box. The child who has no brothers or sisters may wonder where those babies are. If they do not appear, he worries about how his mother is disposing of them. Because children have an utterly disproportionate idea of their own power, they may suppose something they said or did has interfered with babies being born in their family.

When a baby actually arrives, these unconscious worries tend to be relieved. "See, babies are getting born. Everything is all right anyway," becomes an unspoken thought that helps to make coexistence with the baby more bearable.

Probing a child's unconscious fears and wishes is no part of a parent's or a teacher's job. This is a field which can be left to the well-trained professional, when and if a child is in difficulties. Yet it is helpful to be aware that unconscious feelings do exist and do have an influence.

WHEN NEW BABIES ARE APPEALING

For the girl who is anywhere from six to ten, a new baby in the family has a different meaning than it would have had when she was somewhat younger. During these years, girls for all their tomboy ways are usually interested in imitating their mothers. Whether the baby born during this period of a girl's life is the second child, or whether more babies have come along in the intervening years, she is apt to be pleased with the newcomer. Much of the time she is likely to be helpful and almost protective with her mother—when there is not too much afoot with her own friends.

Girls go through a stage of feeling left out similar to that described in *Judy's Baby* by Sally Scott (N.Y., Harcourt, Bruce, 1948). This is, incidentally, a delightful book to read with a seven-, eight- or nine-year-old girl when there is a new baby in the family. Judy at first felt that the baby was a nuisance, but the story relates how her affection and interest blossomed as time went on.

Evelyn Barkins, in her entertaining account of her fourth baby, *Four Children for the Doctor* (N. Y., Frederick Fell, 1954), tells how a ten-year-old daughter tried to take charge of a mother's pregnancy.

"Daddy," Lizzie exclaimed, "We never should have let Mother do any painting Saturday! *In her condition.*"

For the moment John was so shocked that he dropped the roll he had half buttered, and his jaw. "Really?" he gasped, and when he could speak again, "You don't say."

"Yes," said Lizzie dramatically . . . "And her diet's terrible! She doesn't even take Vitamins . . . or calcium either . . . Golly! What sort of bones will our baby have? . . ."

"Now look here, Lizzie," John began, when we had finally managed to stop laughing, "Mother and I had three babies before this. Besides, I'm a doctor . . . Why don't you just relax and forget about the baby until it's ready to arrive?"

"But it's my baby, too!" she said. "I only want to help."

Lizzie was not the only ten-year-old who has undertaken to supervise her mother under such conditions. Lizzie's superior airs undoubtedly stemmed largely from genuine interest, but there may also have been in her mind the common ten-year-old suspicion that one's parents aren't quite bright. Then, too, Lizzie, who already had a younger sister and brother, may have had some unspoken reservations about the desirability of this fourth baby.

School-age boys are less interested in the new member of the family than are their sisters, yet they, too, may enjoy sharing in its care if they see their fathers doing so, and if nobody hints that it is unmanly. Since boys during these years are mortally afraid of appearing to be babyish themselves, or of admitting that they still need their mothers, their resentment against the baby is likely to be masked. An indifference or some of the disguised expressions of jealousy resorted to by younger children may cover their real feelings.

WHEN SCHOOL AGE CHILDREN RESENT A BABY

A new baby is an important event in the life of the eldest, no matter what his phase of development. A child who has had an especially difficult time accepting the brother or sister closest to him in age may have some of his original resentment rekindled with the birth of each baby in the family. Yet, because as he grows up, a wider range of interests and satisfactions have opened out to him, and because he is less dependent on his mother, later babies do not blot out the sun for the first-born as completely as the second child did.

The school-age boy or girl who shows signs of being upset can often be helped by some of the same devices that comfort a younger child. Time spent alone with mother and father in pleasant ways—not in straightening bureau drawers or practicing arithmetic problems—is often the key to improvement. Children of this age respond well as a rule to extension of privileges. Since this is the age of widening horizons and of a great need for achievement, permission to go further on their own in every sense of that phrase means more to them than it does to younger ones. Games and sports, activities in the arts, hobbies, collections, dramatics and puppets enlist their interest and channel feelings of rivalry and resentment.

"I need your help" is a challenge which can, on occasion, bring out a surprising amount of cooperation in the eight- or ten-year-olds. It is a distress call which should be used judiciously and only when the help a youngster can give is visibly necessary and effective.

Girls can often be reached by the "You and I are in this together" appeal from their mothers, if it is not overdone. After all, the baby is the parents' responsibility. Still, girls enjoy feeling they are for the moment on a grown-up level. Boys are likely to respond to the man-to-man approach from their fathers. When cooperation is asked for, let it be in a specific instance. Exacting a promise for something vague like "being good" or being "nice to the baby" usually leads to defeat and confusion.

The grade-school child who seems belligerent or sullen can sometimes talk about his feelings. Attempts to force him to talk when he would rather keep his troubles to himself may result in a grimmer silence, but when he is ready to sound off, a parent can be a sympathetic listener. Doubtless it will be just at the moment when the gravy is starting to thicken or when a mother has an armful of clothes that must be put away. Children seem to choose the most inopportune times for their confidences. "If I can get Mom to listen to me now, that means she really cares," may be one form of reasoning. "Dad won't start lecturing if he's fixing the car," may be another.

Knowing that his feelings are neither unique nor alarming, and that others, perhaps even his own parents, have as children resented new babies is as reassuring, and as surprising, to a seven- or nine-year-old as to a younger child.

NEW BABIES AFFECT TEEN-AGERS, TOO

Growing older does not always mean growing more reasonable. An adolescent, either a boy or girl, may be thrown into considerable turmoil if his parents present him with a brother or sister.

The eldest in a large family may see this new member as a further economic drain. "There goes my chance to go to college," a high school junior bitterly remarked when he was told of the impending arrival of a fifth baby. To a teen-age girl, another baby may well spell more duties, less time to do the things that interest her, less room, and less opportunity to entertain her friends.

Teen-agers may be annoyed even if the family is not large and the baby will not disrupt their lives. Adolescents usually take the stand that whatever their parents do is questionable. A baby is one more piece of evidence that parents are prone to be stupid. Underlying any of these expressed objections is the sometimes unconscious resentment of the baby as indisputable proof of the sexual relations of parents. In this phase of development that fact is unacceptable. "Oh, you don't mean you did *that!*" a thirteen-year-old said to her mother on hearing there would be a fourth baby. "And to think," her mother said in relating the incident, "that her father and I worry about her being so sophisticated."

Then, too, junior high and high school students find it unbearable to differ from their contemporaries. Most of their schoolmates do not have babies at home. One eldest's mother could not attend his graduation from boarding school because a sister was born that week. The boy felt so disgraced that he would not admit why his mother stayed away. "Nobody, but nobody who is anybody has a baby at his house," he protested. The adolescent can, on occasion, be the most reactionary conformist.

Even if he is fourteen or sixteen years old, an eldest wants to feel his parents are interested in him despite the baby. His attitude of "I don't need anything from you" is deceptive. Parents can still be available to discuss plans for a party, for next year's courses, or this summer's job, if they are lucky enough to be consulted.

An infant in the house may seem to a mother like a renewal of her own youth, while a six-foot son or a curvaceous daughter is a not-so-welcome reminder that she is no longer twenty-nine. The eldest still needs his parents. In some ways he needs their emotional support as keenly as he did ten years ago.

WHAT DOES THE ELDEST MEAN TO THE BABY?

Relationships are two-way streets. While the eldest is struggling to accept the fact that there is a younger member of the family, that younger one is forming a picture of himself as a person with an older brother or sister as well as parents. How the older one looks to him will depend on the older one's age and the way he treats the baby.

The achievements of the more accomplished individual are at once a spur and a solace to the younger one. He feels urged on, but not goaded to the unattainable as he watches the elder. When the older child can begin to teach the younger one what to do, he takes pride in him, at least he does so in those moments when he is not pushing the smaller one down. Even when the eldest is doing that, he is probably somewhat proud of his brother or sister.

One father said he could date the beginning of the comrade-liness between his two daughters who are just a year apart in age. When the younger one was crawling, the elder was just under two. She would get down on the floor and crawl with her sister, push-ing and pulling her to the chair where their father sat. "This is Daddy. Say 'hi, Daddy'," she would insist. After this performance had been repeated many times, the younger really did say "Hi." The older girl was immensely pleased with herself as a teacher, and with the discovery that baby sisters could be fun.

Some babies whose brothers or sisters are two or three or five years older learn to hang on tightly to whatever they have. As soon as they can stand up, they duck when anyone comes near them. They have been shoved down and had things snatched away from them so frequently that they consider that to be the way of the world. Most of them bob up and come back for more. Their devotion to the slightly older child may seem to have little reason behind it, but he is their hero and their model anyway.

In the interests of the welfare of both, and of their later rela-tionship, the smaller needs some protection, but probably not so much as tender-hearted parents believe.

GRANDPARENTS—ALLIES FOR THE ELDEST

For the boy or girl who is getting less of mother's attention than he thinks he should have, grandparents can be an especial asset. The eldest in the family is likely to be a favorite with his grand-parents. Having favorites is among the luxuries granted to a grandmother and a grandfather. If in addition to being the eldest of his own parents, he is the first grandchild in the family, a pre-ferred position is all but assured.

Giving a child an extra measure of love is the greatest contribu-tion grandparents make. Another aspect of this same gift is that they can lighten the darker days in the eldest's life. Before a mother has become accustomed to managing two children, grand-parents may have more time to spend with the older one than a mother has.

Grandparents usually enjoy their grandchildren more if they

can have them one at a time. This plan is gratifying to the eldest, for if there is a baby or two at home, he may need to get away from it all occasionally.

If a father's or mother's own parents are not available, a substitute set of grandparents who are keenly aware of their loss in not having their own grandchildren near by will repay cultivation. They will probably be eager to make up for their lack and both families will benefit.

FUTURE RELATIONSHIPS ARE AT STAKE

In an earlier day, when a small child showed signs of resentment toward a new baby, the recommended course of action was "Pay no attention to him. He'll get over it." Now we appreciate that a new baby is a real crisis for the eldest. More is involved than getting rid of immediate undesirable behavior. An eldest needs help and encouragement in his efforts to find ways of living with the new baby and with himself, without too great a strain most of the time. If that goal can be achieved or even approximated, the foundation for a fundamental loyalty, warmth, and regard for the younger children in the family has usually been laid. More than that, a basis for meeting new situations, accepting change, and sharing when that is necessary, without being seriously threatened, may also have been established.

Parents can take the longer view and ask themselves: "How will this boy or girl feel about his brother or sister two years or twelve years from now?" "How will this youngster meet difficult situations five or ten or twenty years hence?"

The goal is to have a child understand that while things may often be hard, still you can turn to others for help. We want our children to grow up feeling "There are strengths within me. I can cope with these things. There are friendly and sympathetic people in my world."

CHAPTER V

The Eldest and His Brothers and Sisters

What does it mean in respect to getting along with the other children in the family to be the eldest among them? How can we help a first child play his part with brothers and sisters so that each may profit by the others varied abilities and good qualities rather than constantly pitting their strength against one another? How can we handle the tensions and cultivate the friendliness inherent in the relationship of the children?

THICKER THAN WATER

Every parent who grows discouraged over the lack of cordiality between his eldest and younger ones in the family can take heart from reading Irwin Shaw's story, "Strawberry Ice Cream Soda" (in *Sailor off the Bremen*, N.Y., Random House, 1937), in which the elder teen-age brother Eddie is contemptuous of the thirteen-year-old Lawrence whose chief interest and talent lies in playing the piano. An incident arises in which Lawrence refuses to accept the challenge to fight with a boy his own age. The older brother feels disgraced by this defection, but when a few minutes later Lawrence does fight, this conversation takes place between Eddie and the father of the other combattant.

" 'Say,' said the farmer, 'do you think your brother'll damage my kid?'

" 'It's possible,' Eddie said. 'He's very tough . . . One day Larry fought three kids all in a row . . . He's got a terrific left jab . . . and it gets 'em in the nose.' "

The younger brother emerges with his face battered but his honor intact.

"The two brothers walked away, close together . . . they walked in the silence of equals, strong men communicating in a language more eloquent than words."

Eddie in his pride in Lawrence's performance, spends the thirty-five cents he had saved for his first date that night for the strawberry ice-cream soda Lawrence had been begging for earlier in the afternoon.

The kindlier feelings such as Eddie displayed are present, but one needs to be aware of the causes of those cross currents of resentment and of affection which show up daily between the children. A strong force making for warmth and understanding is the tendency in human beings to copy the feelings of those with whom they live. As the children feel themselves a part of one another, or identify themselves one with another, the bond between them grows firmer. They develop the capacity to put themselves in one another's place. What brings enjoyment to one can (even if it only occasionally does) give satisfaction to a brother or sister. Sorrows and set-backs that come to the eldest are shared sometimes by the younger children. Younger ones bask now and then in the reflected glory of the big brother or sister. A sharing and a contagion of feelings, pleasant and unpleasant, is a two-way proposition between elder and younger. It is evidenced in the five-year-old who cries if her smaller sister is scolded, as well as in the triumph of the seven-year-old when his oldest brother makes the team.

A second tie between the children grows out of the sense of having been through much together. The common background, the shared traditions, the ability to find the same things in the present as well as the past amusing or touching draws together those who have grown up under the same roof.

THE ANATOMY OF RESENTMENT

In spite of the strength of the forces drawing brothers and sisters together, several causes of rivalry and resentment operate from time to time to set them against one another. Two reasons why resentment is prominent have already been discussed. First, every child wants to possess his parents completely, and is indignant with anyone who interferes with such possession. A second cause of conflicts is that friendliness and unfriendliness exist at almost the same moment in everyone.

The sharing and giving that are demanded as children learn to live together in the family constitute a third cause of the friction between them. To a child, it is infinitely more blessed to receive than to give. Yet give the eldest must, as he soon discovers in his contacts with a brother or sister. The sharing of such tangibles as toys or candy bars or even the best place at the window if something particularly fascinating is going on outside is difficult but not unbearable. Expediency and a desire to please eventually dictate that it is prudent not to hang on too tightly or inflexibly to what one has at the moment. The pressure to take turns is strong in every group, though the young individualist resists it. If not at four or five, then somewhat later most children grasp the rudiments of the idea that turnabout is the rule.

The kind of giving that is learned more slowly but that is essential to a deeper relationship has to do with intangibles. The capacity to share the affection and attention of someone you love, to take into consideration the needs of another person, to give up something you want for the sake of another, develops in two-steps-forward, one-step-backward fashion. In a clumsy manner children can practice this kind of giving within the family.

The ultimate goal is a true concern for another person's welfare and happiness. The absence of that kind of concern, even in adults who supposedly possess it, is pointed up in a story—probably legendary—about a famous, but egotistical musician. Meeting a friend on the street, he discoursed at length on his own recent orchestral triumphs. "But here," he said, "We've been talking about me. Now, you must tell me, what's been happening to you. How did you like my last concert?"

Such self-centeredness, absurd in an adult, is quite natural in a child. His capacity to be concerned about someone else is typified by the three-year-old's reply when his mother said, "I'm writing to grandma. Do you want to tell her something?" The answer was, "Tell her she should bring me a present."

A fourth cause of ill-feeling among the children in the family is the competitiveness rampant in most homes and throughout society today. Whether its germ is the rivalry between children for their parent's affection or whether that rivalry only mirrors the "anything you can do, I can do better," spirit of the outside world is beside the point. Both are here to stay, and each heightens the other. The problem is how to keep family life from being reduced to a perpetual race.

A fifth and more obvious reason why the eldest and his brothers and sisters do not always get along well is that they are so continually treading on one another's toes. Living in close quarters, youngsters jostle one another at every turn. The child with a chip on his shoulder is sure to get it knocked off frequently. Eldest children often do carry such chips. In their turn, they are quick to trip up, both figuratively and literally, a younger member of the family.

In what other relationship short of serving a sentence are you so much in the company of someone not of your own choosing or from whose company no release or transfer is in sight?

THE EXAMPLE FOR THOSE WHO FOLLOW

When mothers in a parent education discussion group were asked, "What do you think it means in relation to the other children in the family to be the eldest?" these were among their answers:

"It means to have been displaced."

"It means to have to give to others more than they will give to you."

"You have to be the example to the younger ones."

"You think that you are the king pin and everyone who isn't a grown-up is smaller and less important than you."

"You are afraid somebody will oust you and you never feel secure."

"The eldest has to take responsibility and be a stand-in for the parents."

"The oldest is always afraid the next one may catch up with him."

"More is expected of the oldest when he is still little."

"If you are the first, you are treated more like an adult, and at least to the younger ones, you look pretty grown up, and they look hopelessly babyish to you."

"You not only have to be good, you have to be irreproachably good. What I hated when I was a child was that I was supposed to be such a model of industriousness and politeness that even if my sisters fell short of the example I set, they would still be passably well-behaved."

When junior high school students were asked how they felt about being the oldest in their families, these were among their answers:

"When you're the oldest you're supposed to set an example. I like that, it keeps me on my toes."

"If I don't make a good record at school or if I'm not called a good kid on the block, my little brothers are going to suffer for it. They'll be judged by what I do."

"I was always the big girl who was supposed to know better and not get into trouble or let the little ones get into trouble. That kind of gave me some purpose for trying to do the right thing. I think its been good for me and good preparation."

"When you're oldest you get blamed if the younger ones don't turn out right."

"I'm glad I'm oldest, because at school or at camp or in Scouts, I can just be myself and make my own record. It just happens that I got good marks in school. It's going to be tough for my brother, because he'll be expected to live up to what I did. Now if he'd been first, I'd have a hard time living his record down. If our little sister had been first, that would have been still worse, because she's really sharp."

"My younger brothers say to me, 'Everywhere we go we're just

Elmer's little brothers. We get sick of hearing your name all the time'."

Being the example appears to be the common denominator when adults and young people count the blessings—or the penalties—of being eldest. Serving as a model is often the source of the eldest's resentment or of the reciprocal annoyance younger ones feel toward him. We can see here a directive for us, as adults, who have charge of children at home, at school or in informal groups: play down the competition and comparisons. What is gained by offering an incentive is lost by creating antagonism.

In spite of the widespread conviction that the family honor rests on the shoulders of the eldest, let us not make that honor too burdensome. We can resist the temptation to call attention to the fact that the first-born is the standard bearer.

In a curious way the oldest is for parents, too, a prototype. The first child, to a greater extent than other children he has known, shapes a parent's ideas of what youngsters are likely to do and of how they grow. Later children are inevitably looked upon as "faster" or "slower," "even cuter" or "less good looking" than the first one. No matter how earnestly mothers and fathers promise themselves not to make comparisons, the first child has set a pattern.

Whether the first-born is likely to be brighter or less bright than later children has been the subject of numerous studies whose conflicting findings establish at least one fact: the experiences of some eldest children tend to make them appear more advanced intellectually, yet in individual families it is safer not to make up one's mind ahead of time as to how the children will turn out.

THE PAVER OF THE WAY

Paving the way for the other children starts with birth itself. As in the process of birth, so in other strenuous efforts, the eldest often makes things easier for those who follow him. This is an aspect of their position many first children resent. Gwen Raverat, in her autobiography, *Period Piece* (N.Y., Norton, 1953), discusses how she as the eldest was the victim of some of her parents' theories.

As we grew older, our moral fiber was weakened by having either jam or very heavy dough-cake for tea. But . . . never both. However, this relaxation was the beginning of the end; under our continual pressure the food laws wore thinner . . . till by the time we got down to Billy,—who is nine years younger than I am,—there were no regulations left at all. . . . I cannot see that he is any the worse for it; in fact he is probably less greedy than I am. Ah, innocent child, he little knew how much he owed to my self-sacrificing campaign for liberty, equality and fraternity over the victuals!

Eldest children like Mrs. Raverat often contend that they have fought for larger allowances, more liberal policies on dates, dress, hospitality, and the use of the car, and that the younger ones never appreciate their pioneering. Some parents have found it effective to treat these objections lightly, and to admit that some slight mistakes may have been made in the direction of severity. There is less satisfaction for a teen-ager in complaining about the injustices done him when his parents agree with him and point out that his annoyance is a long standing cross of eldests. A parent's acknowledgement of his fallibility need not become abject apology, but such admission can reduce an adolescent's scornful badgering of younger brothers and sisters in which the real targets are the parents.

Do eldest children really suffer more from overprotection than their juniors? One investigation that set out to test this popular assumption found that the second child gets a sum total of more solicitous care than the first. The second's is more consistent, for while the first child receives more solicitude to begin with, there is a sharp drop when the second arrives. This is another aspect of family relations in which the results of research are at variance. Since parents are dealing with the feelings of their sons and daughters, the problem is not to prove a point, but to help these children realize that their complaints are not unusual and that they have not been handicapped by minor restrictions real or fancied.

BROTHERS ARE A SPUR

How the children in the family get along together depends somewhat on the combination of ages and sexes, but even more on how temperaments of the children affect and interact with each other. One recent study has pointed out that if the next to the eldest in age is of the opposite sex, the eldest may be stimulated to greater efforts, but also feel somewhat insecure.

One section of this same study has given good grounds for the wish often expressed by both eldest boys and girls: "Sure I like being oldest, but if I could have it anyway I wanted, I'd choose to have an older brother." On tests of such mental traits as alertness to details and power of observation, children who were five and six years old, with a brother separated in age by two to four years, did better than those with a sister equally separated in age. When there was a greater age difference, those with brothers were rated relatively high in competitiveness, leadership, and a tendency to insist on their rights, as compared with those who had sisters separated by a similar age span. Brothers, either older or younger seemed to induce more ambition, enthusiasm, and less wavering in decision than sisters, among the children who were tested.

The interesting point is that boys do not consistently excel girls in any of these traits. Yet either boys or girls with a brother seem challenged to use their powers of observation and discrimination more fully than either boys or girls with sisters. Perhaps boys, because they tend to be livelier even at an early age, are more stimulating to other children in the family. Perhaps the other children are more alert, or are more irritated or more jealous of these brothers and, therefore, develop their own powers of self-defense.

A French guidance clinic analysed the cases it had handled to see if the combination of ages and sexes among the children in a family had any bearing on a child's problems. One of the conclusions they reached was that younger brothers are more troublesome than younger sisters. This adds up to the same thing as the study in the United States, except that what the French psychologists label as troublesome we are inclined to accept as being lively, on the alert, or a spur to ambition. This difference in interpretation recalls what the French themselves say in their philosophical way, "Plus ça change, plus c'est la même chose!"

WHEN "ELDEST" EQUALS "ABLEST"

If the first boy or girl is the one to whom things come easily, while the younger ones have more of a struggle; or if there is great divergence in ability in favor of the eldest, the situation is usually not intolerable but needs watching.

When the oldest overshadows the others, he can often be encouraged to use surplus energy in activities that bring him into contact with children outside the family who will not put up with such dominance. An eldest, who is too much the crown prince or princess at home, because of the double advantage of age and an extra measure of ability, needs the company of his or her equals. Group activities under good supervision in Scouts, Camp Fire Girls, church groups, or community centers often drain off into creative channels the energy that might otherwise be expended in ordering the younger children about. The fine old technique of providing such a boy or girl with a lively pet has been known to divert officiousness, too.

WHEN THE OTHERS OUTSTRIP THE ELDEST

When a younger child outdistances the oldest, the situation is more complicated. This was the problem in the Morgan family. Isabel Morgan was a good, steady girl who could be depended upon to straighten her room before she went to school and not to forget what day she had a music lesson. Isabel might have been pretty had she not had so sullen an expression, or if you had not seen her next to her sparkling younger sister, Rita.

When the girls were two-and-a-half and four, Isabel was given a set of six simple puzzles. While she attempted to fit the pieces of one together, Rita worked the other five. That was the story of Isabel's life at every turn. With the younger girl's quicksilver temperament, it was difficult for Mr. and Mrs. Morgan to maintain the seniority rights for Isabel which might have given her status in her own eyes and Rita's. The birth of a brother when Isabel was five only served to put her at a greater disadvantage. Mrs. Morgan grew tired of encouraging her older daughter to join in family activities or the play of other children, for her answer would be, "I don't want to go. I might as well stay home." This attitude grew more pronounced with the years.

Because Isabel could not win approval through the achievements most grade school girls enjoy, and because she had so few satisfactions, she turned to chocolate malteds and candy bars for solace. Being overweight and ungainly made matters worse for her.

When Mrs. Morgan brought Isabel to the office of the family doctor for her annual check up the year she was eleven, he suggested to Mrs. M. that the diet and exercise he was prescribing for her daughter was only a small part of what was needed. He recommended the Morgan's take Isabel to the mental health clinic in a neighboring community.

The worker at the clinic encouraged Isabel to talk about her feelings toward Rita and her brother. In a variety of ways she was able to make it clear to the girl that slower, steadier people are as valuable and likeable as the faster ones who never need to make an effort, and that girls are as valuable and as much of an addition to the family as boys. Isabel, after several months of treatment, began to take fresh courage.

At the same time Mrs. Morgan was seeing another member of the clinic staff. Through interviews with her Mrs. Morgan arrived at a new understanding of Isabel's difficulties. The clinic worker suggested that Isabel's interest in food might be turned to good account. Mrs. Morgan let her older daughter take more responsibility for preparing simple dishes at home.

The Morgans began to look for occasions to praise Isabel's dependability, rather than allowing her slowness to be a subject for family ridicule. Since a month at a summer YWCA camp was not beyond the family's means, the worker opened up that possibility to Isabel's parents.

Isabel went to camp, where none of the girls was aware she had a sister who was smarter and quicker than she. Her counselor, briefed by the camp director, made a real effort to find activities Isabel would enjoy and to draw her into them.

Isabel lost four pounds and gained considerable self-respect. When she returned home, she chattered about the joys of camp and the charms of the counselors. Rita began to regard her with more interest. After all, her older sister had been away on her own, and now had something to say for herself. Mrs. Morgan suggested that Isabel might, with some help, brighten up the glassed-in porch off the kitchen and use it for her own room, so she would have space enough for her camp pictures and mementoes.

An eleven-year-old is not made over in a month, but camp plus the help of the clinic, plus the prestige of her new room and the fact that her parents were showing more approval of her gave Isabel enough self-assurance to join the activities of her classmates. As life seemed less drab, her envy of Rita decreased. Somewhat slow Isabel would probably always be. Dash and gayety she might never possess, but she was rescued from being "Pokey old Izzy," and gradually became "The girl whom we can count on."

The eldest may be at a disadvantage in the pre-adolescent period, not through lack of ability or because he is a less lively personality but merely because he grows at a different pace than the brother or sister close to him in age. The younger may make the big spurt in growth which comes with puberty before the eldest does, if there is only a year or a year-and-a-half between them. If the younger is a girl and the elder a boy, this is likely to happen, since girls mature at an earlier age. For an eldest brother to have his sister towering above him, going out on dates— or clamoring to do so—while he shows few signs of attaining manhood is a bitter blow.

Parents can help such a boy by keeping some seniority rights for him, by interpreting the fact that girls develop at an earlier age, and by pointing out other instances of this same occurrence. Above all they can avoid letting the disparity in size be a subject for ridicule. If there is an opportunity for the children to get away from each other for an extended visit during the summer, or by allowing one to go to camp, the strain may be lessened. A boy will tend to worry less about his own development if his parents do not view the situation as unusual or alarming, but express a cheerful confidence that he will overtake and surpass his sister in size, even while they admit the awkwardness of the present situation.

If a younger sister begins wearing make-up and being interested in boys, and has attained a desirable and shapely femininity, while the elder is still flat of chest and thick of waist line, the competition and jealousy between the two may get out of bounds.

The best that parents can hope to do is make the situation bearable for the first child by letting her feel she is acceptable and by encouraging her to make the most of the things she likes to do. There is a nice balance to be achieved between not pushing her in the direction of a false sophistication for which she is not ready, and yet letting her feel that before long she, too, will attract boys. Emphasis on the fact that some girls have their best years in the early teens, and some have the most fun when they are eighteen or nineteen may seem to be rejected as cold comfort by the girl herself, but it is a valid approach which, in time, makes an impression.

A mother can at least avoid, with an eldest who is as yet not a social success, any unfavorable comparison with the younger sister, or with her own youth.

Separation during vacations may be good for both the girls. Holding the younger back, in the name of fairness to her sister, does not improve their relationship. The emphasis can be on helping the older one find satisfactions in her life, and on letting her feel she is a person who is likeable and valued and will come into her own.

SPECIALISTS IN THE FAMILY

In almost every family, but more conspicuously in a large one, there is some degree of specialization among the children. Each is subtly, though usually unintentionally, assigned a position in the group. The eldest son is frequently cast in the role of protector. An eldest daughter is frequently the maternal or the dominating one.

Before any definite characteristics have appeared, one or both parents may more or less unconsciously decide a child will have a particular kind of personality or behave in a certain way. This judgment may be made on the basis of what happened in their own families, or perhaps what they wished had happened. How this works out was discussed in Chapter II. In any case, a child's picture of himself includes, or is largely made up of, this part he is expected to play. Much of his activity springs from an attempt to live up to what he feels is expected of him, or an effort to get away from the role imposed on him.

Stressing the differing contributions of the children can be a means of cutting down rivalry, too. The attitude that "all these talents are needed. Where would we be without our handyman, our artist, our sociable member, etc.?" lets each child know he is important because he is himself. He is then less driven to be a copy of somebody else. He who knows he is liked and who likes himself is better able to let others have their good points without being corroded with jealously.

Parents or teachers or group leaders can take care not to restrict the part a child plays so greatly that he feels he can do that one thing and no other. Strengths can be emphasized as stepping stones to other achievements, and other desirable attitudes. "You are the kind of person who is good at this, so you can probably do thus and thus also," is a more encouraging stand than "Oh, you, all you can do (or all you are good for) is so and so, better leave that to your sister." The part of the inept one or the dullard need not fall to the lot of any of the children.

ALL OF A KIND

An oldest boy with several younger sisters, or a girl with younger brothers, may need some special provision. Parents can make it clear when there is a minority of one, that both sexes are important. This can come about as the preferences of each are taken into consideration and plans are made with an eye to the needs of each. One girl among a group of boys, or a boy among several girls can be encouraged to enjoy the company of contemporaries of his or her own sex.

The oldest girl may become so much her mother's right hand that she does not have as much time for child-like pursuits with other girls as should, by rights, be hers. If household jobs are classified as women's work, the one girl may be doing tasks that had better be distributed among the boys as well. Genuinely devoted to her brothers though such a girl may be, parents can be careful that this devotion is not exploited and that she does not wait on them hand and foot.

An oldest sister may find competing with three or four brothers taxing. They may be scornful of her because she is only a girl. She needs to have associations in which girls are not at a disadvantage. To grow up feeling that the highest praise is "you are almost as good as a boy," may make it harder to accept one's role as a woman.

Some eldest sisters with several younger brothers are looked up to and beloved. This is particularly true in a family where the mother has died or for some reason is often inaccessible. Kathie, in Brendan Gill's *The Day the Money Stopped* (Garden City, Doubleday, 1957) is an illustration of this, as her brother points out when they are in middle life:

"Thank heaven you and Dick have never had to compete for anything."

"If that's intended as a joke, it's no joke. What have we not competed for. . . ? Including Dad's love and yours? . . . Each of us wanted you to love him more, remember? Or have all those fearful contests over you gone straight out of your mind? How if he climbed onto the roof of the house, I had to climb the chimney? How if I swam twenty yards under water . . . he had to swim thirty? All to woo our dear elder sister and for a long time almost mother."

"That was when you were children, but you stopped being children. We all did, ages ago."

"You flatter us."

An eldest boy with a number of sisters also needs to have his rights protected. Too much emphasis on being gentle and restrained when he is small, too much serving as protector and escort for the sisters as they grow up, can interfere with a boy's essential pursuits. He needs the company of other boys both in his own home and in groups away from home. He will profit, too, from the support and companionship of a father who understands that femininity is not particularly attractive to a boy of six or eight or ten years, but who does not write women off as nuisances himself. A father can offer an escape from feminine talk in ball playing, fishing trips, or working with tools.

Constant restrictions resulting from his minority status can prejudice a boy against women. If he sees them as creatures who must be deferred to, he may have difficulty in overcoming a distaste for girls and all they represent.

One of the great gains in a family of brothers and sisters is that each sex learns to understand and to get along with the other. This end can be accomplished more effectively if neither sex is disregarded nor highly favored.

WHEN CONFLICT IS COMMUNICATION

No matter how parents try to maintain an atmosphere that makes for friendliness, there is sure to be some open resentment in the form of quarreling, tattling, and teasing between the eldest and the other children. The younger children reciprocate the eldest's annoyance and rivalry, and less obviously, his affection, too. While open conflict may not take so great an emotional toll as the kind that is disguised sometimes does, still when it is rampant, the wear and tear on everyone is great. How shall clashes be handled?

Parents often wonder what is "too much" in the matter of squabbles. Each family has its own tolerance for angry words and blows. What might be branded as total family warfare in one household may pass for a slight skirmish in another. How much mothers and fathers permit depends on what those arguments, or out-and-out fights, mean to them and what they mean to the children involved.

Mothers especially need to keep in mind that children are neither precise nor polite in their language. "Dope," "stinker," "dirty rat," and as one five-year-old fancied it "some of a gun" in the context of youthful interchange are not the fighting words they become when adults use them.

QUARRELSOMENESS—SYMPTOM NOT SIN

Controversies between the children are not entirely due to three of them wanting the same chair, or block, or apple at the same time. These battles over anything, or nothing, have several components.

Interwoven with strong feelings about the immediate cause are recollections for each child of other times this brother or sister has bested him. The deep-lying root of the quarrel is the long-standing competition for a mother's and father's favor. Here is a clue to why there is more fighting in the presence of parents than when someone else is in charge.

He who is the aggressor may need more affection and comfort, rather than punishment and disgrace. A four-year-old or six-year-old who takes a toy away from his brother and beats him over the head with it, needs to be stopped, but he does not need to be told he is a bad boy. Parents can be sure they have the facts before they start to administer justice. Maybe the angel-faced younger one had committed his own particular brand of assault and outrage. Too often, we assume the eldest is wrong because we expect so much control from him. Perhaps, too, the younger one has discovered that the best defence is a great hullabaloo which makes him appear to be the innocent victim when no injury has been done him. The maxim that when a child is most unlovable he most needs loving is the key to the situation.

The fewer times a mother or father feels called upon to step in when trouble has broken out, the better, unless there is actually danger to life and limb. The time for intervention is during the build up of the fight. Suppose a mother knows that her two-year-old, her four-year-old and her five-year-old can manage alone in the back yard for just so long without getting into a major argument or some mischief. She may save time if she makes the trip to the yard, even from a third floor walk-up, to see whether a suggestion for a new twist to their play, a few words of approval, or a cracker for all hands can turn the rising tide of tension.

"Conductors on trains have to take care of the passengers. Conductors who push them around lose their jobs," may be a more cogent reason for not mistreating a sister than any appeal to chivalry or fairness.

"Somebody has to be gate keeper if you're playing zoo. Why don't you make Robby the man who stands at the gate?" can get Robby into the game without preaching at his older brother.

"Real farmers ride one at a time on their tractors. You can have more fun that way," does not interrupt the flow of the children's play and appeals to them more than safety rules.

Fatigue, hunger, and tedium are great trouble breeders. Planning can often head off an explosion. The minutes that go into such prevention are made up many times over. The children learn more from successful experiences in getting along together than from failures. Good supervision for young children, as can be observed in a well-run nursery school, consists in stepping in to redirect or to prevent clashes, more often than in settling full blown feuds.

Louise Dickenson Rich, in *Only Parent*, (Phila., Lippincott, 1953) gives a touchstone for deciding whether altercations are safely within normal bounds.

Sometimes, though, they surprise me very much. They may be in a fight to end all fights. . . . They may be screaming at each other, and saying how much they hate each other, and spitting and slapping each other like a couple of Kilkenny cats. Tears of rage will be pouring down Dinah's cheeks . . . and Rufus will be taunting her, calling her 'chicken' for crying, and otherwise behaving in an objectionable manner. But if I try to interfere, or the kid next door comes along and wants to make it a three cornered fight, you'd be amazed at how quickly the breach is healed. Dinah moves over to stand beside her brother. . . . Rufus adopts a bull-necked "Oh? Yeah!" stance, and ordinarily they rout the foe without having to fire a single shot, so impressive is their solid front. They may then go right back into their own fight, but usually the spirit has gone out of it. I don't think I'm going to worry too much about their affection for each other.

Not the fights, but the ability to stand together when the occasion arises, not the incidents which set them against each other, but the situations that bring out a degree of even temporary cooperation, bear witness to the potential friendliness between the children in the family. As long as they can make common cause, like Dinah and Rufus, one does not have to worry about their affection for each other.

PROTECTION FROM THE WILES OF THE YOUNGER

The younger child, through sheer charm, may make the elder appear in a bad light. Oliver was his mother's favorite, though she tried to be fair to Florence, his older sister. Oliver, his father maintained, was a moral humbug. When he was four and his sister was seven, she would often neglect her mother's instructions about watering the plants, brushing the dog, or running an errand either promptly or cheerfully.

Then Oliver would look up at his mother and solemnly protest that when he was big he would be so glad to help his mother, and that he would do what his sister had been asked to do right now if he only knew how. If Florence gave her brother a slap or a pinch, or told him stories of giants who cut little boys in pieces, she could hardly be blamed.

A three- or four-year-old boy who is wrapped up in his mother can be a thorn in the side of a sister a few years older. A mother can watch out lest she be taken in by the blandishments of her son and overlook the real efforts her older daughter is making to stay on a good footing with her.

For one reason or another, parents favor now one child, now

another. Not to do so would be superhuman. The parent who can admit to himself he is favoring one and counterbalance that favoritism at times has no need to feel guilty. If a mother is aware that one child is trying to create an effect, as the boy in the preceding example was, she can avoid allowing one child to exploit the other.

LOOK AT THE ROOTS OF TEASING

Teasing is an expression of rivalry which seeks to attack an opponent at his most vulnerable point, either by tearing down that which he prizes or exposing that which he would prefer to hide. Teasing says in effect to its victim, "You are less worthy, less competent, less important than you think you are, or than I am, and I can prove it." It is the weapon of choice for one who would get the better of a competitor who, by his very existence, constitutes a threat.

Sally Benson, in *Junior Miss* (N. Y., Random House, 1939), has created two sisters, Lois and Judy Graves who are adolescent experts in the subtler shades of belittling one another. This scene at breakfast takes place when a shopping expedition is anticipated.

"Good morning, Judy," her mother said.

Across the table, Lois smiled and her eyes closed like a cat's.

"Well, Judy," her father said, "I hear you're going shopping to-day!"

She sighed. "I suppose so."

"You *suppose* so," Lois jeered. "She hasn't been able to eat for a week!"

"Mother," pleaded Judy, "does she have to go with us?"

"She does," Mrs. Graves answered. "Now, not so early in the morning girls, please."

As Judy helped herself to 2 tablespoons of sugar, Lois shook her head meaningly. "Better watch yourself," she said. "Not that it isn't too late, P.K."

P.K. meant Powerful Katinka.

"You're getting too old to tease your sister every minute, Lois," Mrs. Graves said.

"Fifteen isn't so old," Judy scoffed. "She tells everyone she's sixteen. Fifteen is just a baby age really."

"If I'm a baby, what does that make you?" Lois asked.

"Quiet or you both stay home," Mrs. Graves said.

The classic cause of teasing is envy of the brother or sister who stands too well with parents, who is held up as a model, or who is thought to be better looking, brighter, or more fortunate.

A logical measure might seem to be subjecting the offender to a dose of his own medicine. Since the inveterate teaser is acting out his resentment or his boredom, to increase his discomfort by teasing him makes matters worse. Not doing unto others what you do not want them to do to you, particularly if they are not capable of doing it, is an ethic few children can comprehend.

A parent's teasing, for purposes of retaliation, appears to a child to be an unwarranted attack. When adults stoop to his methods, a child is outraged. He wants to feel his parents can accomplish their ends in a better way. Teasing a nine-year-old to "show him how it feels," is as ineffective as hitting a two-or three-year-old to teach him not to do that.

Teasing is often acute in homes where competition is made a tool for discipline, where severity is the rule and parental favor is conditional upon good behavior or satisfactory marks in school. The adults themselves may be setting an example of more sarcasm and teasing than they realize. Indirect means of reducing the teasing by getting at its cause is in the long run more helpful than prohibiting it or punishing the offender.

RETREAT MAY HIDE RESENTMENT

Troublesome as signs of open resentment may be, they are more easily dealt with, and more easily recognized, than resentment in disguise. Some eldest children who have discovered in their earliest days that retreat and renunciation are more likely to win favor than louder forms of protest are unconsciously afraid to let their rivalry or anger come in the open.

Harry was such a boy. His grandparents shared his parents' home, and quietness was the prime virtue in their eyes. Then came in quick succession a sister and two brothers for Harry. Not showing anger, not putting himself forward or competing continued to be the qualities that earned approval. In these qualities Harry excelled. When he willingly relinquished to one of the younger ones his cookie, or his toy engine, or a penny that had been given him for staying out of the way, he would be praised by the adults in the house. When he stood up for his own rights, he was likely to be sharply reprimanded, particularly if he won his point. As this situation was repeated, time after time, Harry learned one lesson—it is not worth getting what you want. If you succeed, everyone is down on you. Harry's conscience would bother him if he got his own way just as it did if he had done something on the long list of forbidden, and albeit harmless, acts.

Harry grew up afraid to compete. He was afraid to learn when he went to school. "You can only be loved if you are helpless," had been demonstrated to him. Who is so helpless as he who repeatedly fails? As the three younger children became more healthily self-assertive, he became more and more anxious to avoid disputes with them.

Harry never seemed able to see anything through to its conclusion. When success lay within his grasp, he would usually manage to make a misstep. He was eager to play the drum in the school band when he was twelve, but he forgot to go to the final tryout. Another year his painstakingly prepared collection of shells mysteriously disappeared the day before he was to display it at the boys' club hobby show. For the most part, none of these episodes worried his parents as long as Harry was not fighting or arguing with his younger sister and brothers.

As a result of a childhood spent in proving he wanted nothing, although his life was not marked by major tragedies, he was dogged by failures and found few satisfactions.

Had Harry been given the feeling, "You can be loved, even though you fight back," "You can get the best of somebody else without becoming an outcast," he would not have needed to pull into his shell for fear of getting involved in any conflict.

A child like Harry needs to know, too, that it is not bragging to say one can do something well. Harry would insist, "I don't know how" or "I don't think I could do that," when he knew he could.

Here was a boy who would have profited by a sense of mastery gained through using tools and wood or playing a musical instrument like the drum. Intuitively he had known that would be a release. Such activities would have fostered self-respect and afforded a safety-valve for some of his repressed anger. Harry was the type of boy often successfully treated at a child guidance center. Because parents and teachers see no problem in a child who is never troublesome, these boys and girls frequently do not get the help they need.

One means of letting a child know that there are many good ways of getting along with people, some appropriate at one time, some at another, is through family games. Boys and girls between the ages of six and twelve enjoy variations on the checkers or parchesi type of game with penalties and rewards. Outdoor games in which you must touch home base before you are caught in order to be safe are favorites too. Through playing such games at home, children find out that it is not dangerous to win today anymore than it was cataclysmic to have lost yesterday. These experiences often illustrate without any preaching that both winning and losing have a place.

TOWARD FRIENDLIER RELATIONS

The youngster who is far too self-effacing or far too eager for the limelight, who is a perfectionist or a scatterbrain, who is clingingly affectionate with adults on first acquaintance or unwilling to make friends with grown-ups who are genuinely interested in him may harbor intense resentment against his brothers and sisters. This antagonism may be the root of his difficulty. Jealousy drives children to peculiar kinds of behavior as well as makes them competitive or belligerent.

If improvement in the quality of the children's relationship seems to be in order, there are several steps parents and teachers can take. Some of them, such as avoiding comparisons, deemphasizing competition, planning for separate activities, and encouraging dramatic and creative play to drain off resentment, have already been suggested. Devices which help a boy or girl when there is a new sister or brother are equally useful in the later relationship of the children, but any technique must be geared to the age and ability of the boy or girl in question.

Each child is strengthened by knowing that the adults around him are aware of his tastes and interests. In a large family, if two or three are close in age, there is a tendency to lump them together to such an extent that they lose the feeling of being distinct personalities.

"TO DISTINGUISH BETWEEN" IS NOT "TO DISCRIMINATE AGAINST"

Many parents insist they treat the children alike because that is the fair thing to do. Besides, they say, the children will protest if one gets anything slightly different from the others. This is a shortsighted confusion of identical distribution with justice.

The children may complain at first if each is given a different present or if all are not treated in the same manner. If the adults around them make it clear, and are themselves convinced, that distinctions are made because "different people like different things," the children eventually absorb the fact that the distinctions are not discriminatory.

The realization that today a parent may do a special favor for one, but tomorrow he will do the same for another makes for a better spirit than "fairness" measured by the inch. Some parents who would not dream of allowing themselves to be swayed from their own sound judgement in matters of health or discipline are badgered by the children into the rule of "same for everyone," even when the adults know it is not the best procedure.

Another way of avoiding squabbles is by distinguishing between common property such as the sand boxes or the phonograph and individual possessions such as toys, in the early years, or clothes, in later childhood. If children share a room, each can have his own shelf, drawer, or hooks in the closet. Respect for the property of others begins with having some treasured possessions that are entirely one's own. These can be kept in a place no one else is allowed to touch.

Just as parents can tide an individual child over bad moments by discovering what comforts him, so they can often reduce tension by discovering and remembering what activity two or three of their youngsters are able to pursue together with reasonable peace and goodwill. Perhaps it will be looking at pictures, or a TV program, listening to music or dressing up, using a toy or game that is kept for special occasions, or joining forces in making a favorite simple dessert. Knowing that they can put their heads together happily gives them some confidence in their relationship.

One nine-year-old gave evidence of this on a rainy afternoon, just when his mother thought her eardrums would burst. With a sudden spurt of leadership, he announced to his younger brothers, "Say you guys, let's get out that box of old postal cards. Looking at those is something nobody is any worse at than anybody else."

SENIORITY RIGHTS

The core of a teen-ager's problem is to gain independence from his parents and to learn to get along with the opposite sex. Admitting that brothers and sisters are troublesome may be easier than acknowledging the real source of difficulty—a source the teen-agers may not recognize. Yet it is significant that brothers and sisters appear to be the cause of many of their troubles.

One reason why the small ones outrage the teen-ager is that they never let the past be buried. They are ever ready to cut the would-be man or woman-of-the-world down to size. An untimely mention of a big sister's fondness for pillow fights or paper dolls, of an older brother's addiction to caramel apples or carousels can be devastating in the presence of another adolescent, especially of the opposite sex. The comic strips have long featured the small brother who divulges his sister's secrets to her beaux. That situation is so universal that it strikes a responsive chord in most people. An adolescent may be able to convince his parents that he has attained a degree of maturity, but younger brothers and sisters will not accept that fact.

Smaller children disturb the eldest when he or she is studying, listen in on phone conversations, hang around when friends, particularly friends of the opposite sex, are visiting, and use the eldest's possessions without permission. This is the bill of particulars the first-born brings against the younger members of the family. Parents can use both direct and indirect measures to improve matters.

That oft-invoked device, the family council, can be a means of ironing out some of these difficulties. The younger children themselves, if the problem is brought up at a judicious moment, may find a workable solution. Airing points of view on conflicting interests can drive home the fact that other persons have needs and feelings, too. A remark like "Well, if I do listen in on her phone calls, it's because she's always telling me what's wrong with my friends," from a younger sister can remind the elder that there are two sides to these questions. Discussion, even if heated at times, can lead toward a modification of attitudes and actions on the part of both.

In one study when eldests were asked how they would handle the situations of which they complained, the majority of those with three, or fewer, younger brothers and sisters advocated reasoning with the smaller ones. The majority of those with four or more younger ones in the family approved of punishment. To a lesser extent did these eldests feel that the situation could be solved in a cooperative, reasonable way. This might lead one to believe that there is a saturation point beyond which an adolescent cannot tolerate being annoyed and needs to have his rights respected.

What parents hear when they encourage the children to discuss their problems with each other may throw light on the underlying tensions. What the children say may suggest changes which can reduce rivalry so that the younger ones will not become pests. Not rules or punishments but a change in ways of dealing with the children may be the answer. Tension between an adolescent and his brothers and sisters may be intensified by tension between him and his parents, and a certain amount of that is a concomitant of acquiring true independence.

EARMARKS OF A GOOD RELATIONSHIP

As a parent watches his eldest at play and at work with the younger ones in the family, he may wonder what constitutes a good relationship between them.

The relationship between the children needs to be seen in the context of everything else they are doing. A boy or girl of any age who is quarrelsome with younger sisters or brothers, but who can be congenial with children outside the family; who is working up to his capacity at school; who is enjoying life and making progress in growing up may be expected to overcome quarrelsomeness in time. It is probably not a sign of deeper disturbance.

Yet suppose that the same amount of quarrelsomeness were accompanied by a listless attitude in school, habitual sullenness, an avoidance of other children, or an irresistible impulse to lead them into trouble, then the hostilities between the first-born and the rest of the family might be judged one of the signs that he was headed for further difficulties.

Even though a first child may be at odds with the younger ones quite often, parents can afford to take an optimistic view of the matter if he has a variety of ways of tackling his problems and getting along with people. The boy or girl who is able both to give in and to stand firm, to reason things out alone or to accept help, to be enthusiastic or reserved, to enjoy activity or quieter play as the occasions demand is likely to be in a state of emotional well-being. Such a youngster is usually able to respond to steps taken to improve the relationship between the children.

The boy or girl who has only one way of meeting situations, who has no change of emotional pace, and who uses the same approach whether it is serviceable or not is one who needs help from the adults in his life, and perhaps treatment from someone trained in dealing with such problems, as well.

Children who can unite against an outsider, or present a united front to their parents, have a basic relationship to build on. If there are some activities they enjoy together, or if their antagonism decreases markedly when circumstances are especially favorable, the tender shoots of friendliness are not withering away. They just need to be nourished.

If resentment becomes so strong that it pervades every phase of a relationship and every routine day in and day out, or becomes so intense that it interferes with play, school work, or eating or sleeping, then it is time to take stock.

If more affectionate attention, time alone with mother or father, encouragement when a child has fallen short of parental standards or his own, a chance to get away from brothers or sisters, or an opportunity to do those things which give him particular satisfaction, do not improve the situation, then efforts to find qualified professional help may be in order. School counselors, family service societies, mental health associations, or the family's medical or spiritual advisor may offer the kind of help needed.

Relationships between the eldest and his brothers and sisters will take many forms. Whether these forms are helping or hindering an ultimate friendliness cannot be predicted by separating one incident from all those other experiences which impinge on the children. The meaning each experience has for a child depends on his own development at a given moment, and his feelings at the time. The quality of the relationship in the long run weighs heavily in determining the later friendliness and loyalty of these individuals. Fortunately, the hours spent together agreeably, cooperatively, or even cooking up some deviltry counterbalance the hours, or even the days, of bickering and trading insults.

CHAPTER VI

The Eldest Takes Responsibility

When he had described the flowering of the heather, Cordelia, who was older than Mary and me, . . . and made the most of it, sighed noisily and said, "Oh dear! This is going to be a dreadful holiday for me. The children will be wandering off all the time, . . . and getting lost . . . and I will always have to be running after them and bringing them back. And the loch, they are sure to fall into that too."

This was the response of the eldest sister in Rebecca West's *The Fountain Overflows* when the family settled down for a highland holiday.

Being the eldest seems to be synonymous with taking responsibility in the minds of many people, especially those who have occupied that position. What kinds of responsibilities rest on the shoulders of the eldest at different phases in his development? How can we arrange his obligations so that they foster the growth of personality and strengthen his relationship with other members of the family? Why are we so eager to make sure the eldest acquires a sense of responsibility? What signs hint that the first child is being asked to do too much for the others? What do we mean by responsibility? A consideration of these questions can help parents, teachers, or group leaders make the responsibilities that accompany being eldest enriching rather than onerous.

In order to define responsibility, we need to look at the origin of the word. The Latin verb from which it is derived is "to answer" or "to respond." He who is responsible is responsive. To be a responsible individual is to be aware of and concerned with the needs and welfare of others. He carries out directions and assignments most of the time, but, even more important, he puts himself in the other person's place and identifies himself with the other person's feelings. Then he works out a solution and attacks the problem. Those who are responsible tend to be those who are also somewhat conscientious, conforming, and competent. These qualities are prominent in many first children.

A youngster demonstrates his responsibility in two ways. He spontaneously rises to an occasion. He follows through on a task he has undertaken. The task may be one of his own choosing, or one laid out for him. In either case, the stamina to follow through bespeaks a recognition of an obligation and a desire to meet it.

Responsibilities that are peculiarly the eldests' are chiefly caring for the younger members of the family and teaching them the rules and customs of their world. Since the first-born himself is hardly an expert on rules at a tender age, he may pass on a distorted view. The oldest operates mainly as a teacher in this *de facto* and informal schooling of his juniors. Still, learning is a reciprocal affair among the children, even when the senior member of the band is supposedly leading the way. The older may also be learning from the younger.

WHY STRESS RESPONSIBILITY?

Sound reasons, both practical and emotional, underlie the eagerness to have an eldest share in the care of brothers and sisters. On the practical side, the assistance an eldest can give a busy mother may spell the difference between a fairly smooth running household and a pleasant family life, or confusion and pressures. This is increasingly the case as the eldest grows up, the size of the family increases, and a mother has no other source of assistance.

On the emotional side, if responsibilities toward younger children are judiciously assigned and not overwhelming, they provide a way of expressing and strengthening the kindlier feelings of the first boy or girl in the family toward later arrivals. A parent who has decided that too many days of his childhood were spoiled because he had to look after his juniors, and that he will therefore require nothing along that line from his first-born can keep in mind that he may be short-circuiting the wires along which currents of affection and loyalty can flow.

A boy or girl frequently takes over self-appointed tasks in a parent's absence, or *because* of the parent's absence. Even a small child understands the difference between a situation which makes a real demand on him and one in which an adult is in the background and could do the job himself twice as effectively in half the time. Here is one reason why a boy or girl who has been conspicuously unwilling to carry out assigned tasks, which he knows are being allotted to him merely to develop his character, often proves reliable and inventive when the need is acute.

BEING LIAISON OFFICER—EVIDENCE OF CONCERN

The interpretative kind of responsibility is illustrated by the ten-year-old whose younger sister had been suffering from a severe earache. At bedtime the older girl came to her mother and said, "I think Molly is scared. If you'd sleep in my bed in our room tonight, I'd sleep on the couch in the living room. Molly didn't say anything, but I think she'd feel much better if you were right there."

In putting herself in the place of the sick girl, figuring out what could be done, and then interpreting her feelings, the older girl showed reliableness as desirable as that which might have been demonstrated by carrying out a dull task.

In another family, the twelve-year-old sensed a different kind of need on the part of his eight-year-old brother. The father was to be awarded a plaque for his service in community affairs at a formal evening ceremony. The twelve-year-old and his sister, a year and a half younger, were to accompany their parents. The mother and father were hesitant about including the eight-year-old whose deportment at a time of quiet was far from exemplary.

The eldest, a sober boy who usually took a dim view of his brother's antics, was the one who insisted the younger brother be allowed to go, for he declared, "He doesn't have the right respect for you, Dad. He doesn't get much chance to see you in a real favorable light. If he's there when you get this plaque deal, it would be the best thing in the world for him."

In planning for an improvement of his brother's attitude, this boy was taking responsibility for the younger one's behavior and for the family's good name as well.

BEING A PROTECTOR TAXES RESOURCEFULNESS

A five- to ten-year-old may be aware that it is up to him to take over, or to get help if younger members of the family are in trouble. The level-headed action of a nine-year-old boy, entrusted with taking his six- and seven-year-old sisters to school on a public bus, shows how resourceful a youngster that age can be.

One rainy morning the boy had wedged his sisters into the crowded conveyance and stood aside to let an old woman squeeze in. Then the door closed in his face. He stood on the curbstone with the bus fare for the three in his hand. The next stop of this express was the school corner, fifteen minutes away.

To a nine-year-old this was catastrophe. He had visions of the driver dumping the little girls out at an unfamiliar corner or refusing to let them alight with fares unpaid at the stop in front of school. To return home for advice would have meant wasting so much time that he would be late for school and mar the non-tardiness record of his class. He had been brought up in a family where quick thinking stood high on the list of virtues. He had been repeatedly warned never to let the girls out of his sight on the trip to school.

In the drug store, half a block away, he knew there was a phone, and there he headed at full speed. Ten cents of his lunch money went into the phone box, and hurriedly he explained to the secretary at the school what had befallen and insisted that somebody must meet the girls and pay their fares.

Then he ran back to the corner in time for the next express. Fortunately, his resourcefulness was praised at home and at school. His sisters regarded him as nothing short of a savior, and mercifully, nobody pointed out that his measures were unnecessary, for the adults appreciated how extremely responsible he had been.

Eldests do take charge in truly hazardous situations when immediate action is imperative. Two brothers, twelve and fifteen, alone in the house on a cold winter night, awoke to find their second floor bedroom ominously hot and full of choking smoke. The eldest immediately told his brother, Len, to throw pillows and blankets out of the window, while he set to work to knot sheets and secure them to a bedpost. He told Len he would have to go down hand over hand on the sheets and then jump. The younger boy hesitated and begged his brother to go first. The elder one, insisting he would not move until Len was out of the window, boosted him to the window ledge and fairly pushed him off. He waited until he heard his brother drop to the ground, and then went down himself, only seconds before the flames burst through the floor.

The older boy told his father later, "First I thought we ought to do something about the fire, but I saw it was too late for that. For a minute I thought maybe I should go first to show Len it could be done. Then it came to me that if I did, Len might never follow me, so I just shoved him out."

HOW DOES RESPONSIBILITY GROW?

These instances of eldest children who, each in ways appropriate to his age, grasped what needed to be done—or what he was able to do—and acted, pose the question: how does this concern for brothers and sisters and the capacity to comfort or protect them develop?

The foundations of sensitive, resourceful action are laid both directly and indirectly. In a baby's earliest days, as he is on the receiving end of his parents' affectionate care, he feels himself a part of the mother who looks after him tenderly. Gradually, he comes to imitate her feelings and return her love. Exactly how this takes place has not been reduced to a mathematical formula any more than has the process by which leaves turn sunlight into plant food. Yet we know both do occur. As he grows from babyhood into childhood in a home where helping others is the general practice he absorbs some of this attitude without solemn pronouncements being made on the subject.

Still spontaneous responsibility requires more than sympathy and the ability to put yourself in someone else's place. The nine-year-old and the two teen-agers in the stories related above had a problem-solving attitude combined with confidence that bold action is not dangerous. That attitude was the springboard for their behavior.

A child who grows up in a home where his mother and father meet emergencies and setbacks with a degree of resiliency, resourcefulness, and a regard for the facts of the case usually will develop a sense of responsibility.

If this boy or girl has also been given opportunities to practice, in appropriate doses, the solving of his own dilemmas, the outlook for his ultimately becoming a trustworthy individual is favorable. The good results of his experiences and of the atmosphere of his home may show up more vividly in later years.

From discovering that difficulties can be overcome to acquiring the feeling "I can do something about it" is not a big step. That step is made more readily by the child who has also been given the feeling "It is safe to try." One who has been encouraged to use initiative and imagination in his play, and in his efforts to take part and help in the life of the family, more readily becomes a problem solver.

Out of a deep feeling—never put into words—that others have helped and loved me; that I, too, can help people; that something can be done to solve a problem; that I can do it grows the sympathy and the resourcefulness for responsible, spontaneous action on the part of the eldest toward his younger brothers and sisters.

THE BASIC JOBS OF CHILDHOOD

Rising to the occasion may be praiseworthy indeed, but the major concern of parents and teachers and group leaders is in guiding an eldest child so that he will assume the sometimes satisfying, sometimes galling duties toward younger ones in the family which are part and parcel of his daily life.

These continuing responsibilities require perseverance as well as the ability to see and meet a need. Perseverance develops slowly. Even in his own concerns a child does not stick to one activity or stay with one train of thought for an entire afternoon until he is well into the years of middle childhood. Overcoming flightiness is a matter of stronger nerves and muscles, not merely of stronger character. The interrelated flowering of stability and of stamina takes time.

What is a reasonable degree of responsibility for the eldest to assume for the younger children at various phases of his development—and of theirs? In what situations can he be expected to take over or to supplement supervision or give actual routine care?

This question leads to two more basic ones. What is the relationship of the individual to the family in our kind of society? What is the chief business of the growing child?

The essence of democracy is that the state exists for the protection and benefit of the individual citizen. Since family relationships take their color from the wider organization in which they have their being, a youngster is expected to make his contribution to family life, but he does not exist primarily to serve the family. His task is to develop into a well-rounded personality.

Bringing up children is chiefly the parents' responsibility. The continuous care and discipline of a small boy or girl is, literally, not child's play.

A boy or girl between the ages of five and fifteen has his hands full with school and with learning to get along with his contemporaries. Nursemaid duties are a secondary consideration. Not much energy, either physical or emotional, may remain for dealing with a contrary two-year-old, or a rebellious six-year-old after the daily program of a school-age or teen-age boy or girl has been met.

WHEN SHALL RESPONSIBILITIES BEGIN?

The temptation is great to expect a four- or five- or six-year-old either to stay at home so he can keep the still younger ones from straying or getting into trouble, or to require him to take the smaller one or ones with him as he ranges the neighborhood. Under some circumstances this may actually be necessary. If traffic is not heavy, if there is space enough for play and a plethora of play equipment, the eldest may not be burdened by watching out for a younger brother, provided that the younger one is reliable about not running into the street or is not unusually troublesome. The neighborhood and the temperaments of the children—as well as their ages—need to be taken into consideration in allotting this kind of responsibility.

Yet, insisting that the older take the younger along with him may put an undue strain on the younger for keeping up with the older. The older may benefit, too, by the exclusive company of those of his own age with whom he can deal on an equal footing during outdoor play times.

Parents who do not demand a great amount of supervision of the toddlers from an eldest who is under six will probably find the children get along better when they are together. A four-, or five- or six-year-old is struggling to control his own desire to hit and kick. Making adjustments and compromises taxes him to his limits many times a day.

RESPONSIBILITIES THAT CAN BE TAKEN IN STRIDE

How the eldest is managing his own immediate problems is a second point to think about in planning for his care of the younger children. One who is having troubles of his own in school, with his friends, or just in managing his own time may not be equal to looking after younger children when energies are low. An afternoon of play with two or three contemporaries may exhaust the self-control of a seven- or eight-year-old.

If an eldest is unable to take charge of younger brothers or sisters during the pre-supper hour without becoming embroiled in quarrels, it may be possible to let her help in some other way. If she sets the table, cleans the vegetables, or takes over some other task, a mother may be freed to look after the younger children. Tired though a mother may be, she is still more stable than a ten-year-old.

A boy or girl may not be a willing or a careful table setter or vegetable cleaner, but knives and forks and potatoes and carrots will suffer less from rough handling than sisters and brothers. Relationships may improve all along the line, when everyone is tired and tense if the younger ones are not under the direction of the eldest.

The amount of responsibility that can be alloted at a particular time depends also on how much easy companionship exists between the eldest and the other children in the family. A happy youngster who is enjoying most phases of his daily program, and who also enjoys his younger brothers and sisters, can often look after them without much strain.

One such boy, devoted to a sister six years younger who was the third in a family of four, would take her with him and watch out for her under conditions which most youngsters his age would have considered impossible. He was her self-appointed champion and guardian, but he did not assume responsibility for the other two younger ones with any such cheerfulness. One reason why this closeness developed between these two children was that the sister showered on her older brother the admiration and devotion a girl usually gives to her father in her early years. The father in this family was a remote, bookish man, who had not paid much attention to his younger children born late in his own life. The older brother, without anyone realizing it, was taking the father's place.

While the eldest can take more responsibility for the one or ones among his juniors with whom he is most congenial, there may be one member of the family with whom he is for a time at odds and is therefore unable to manage satisfactorily. In that case, it is just as well to arrange matters so that the eldest has fewer tasks in relation to the brother or sister who is a source of irritation.

WHEN RESPONSIBILITIES CAN BE SECONDARY

Sometimes the eldest's duties toward younger children in the family need to be regarded in a special light. Doris was such a case. Doris had been a conscientious thirteen-year-old who seemed to enjoy following her mother's lead as a careful housekeeper and a reliable watcher and washer of her two small sisters. Her brother, close to her in age, was very nearly as independent as Doris and needed no supervision from his sister.

Then the family moved to a new community. The school Doris attended in this town gave her an opportunity to take part in dramatics and in puppet making—activities in which she proved to be talented. She took on an importance with her new school mates and was drawn into a busier, more sociable life than she had known before.

For a time her mother declared good humoredly that she had lost her best assistant, but when Doris had no time whatsoever for the two small sisters, she was definitely displeased.

"What in the world has gotten into you, Dorry? You don't do a thing to help me with your little sisters. Why can't you stay home sometimes on Saturdays the way you used to do in Riverton?" her mother scolded.

"But Mother, when we lived in Riverton I didn't have any friends. Now I can't be bothered with those brats all the time."

Her mother deplored such an attitude toward the younger sisters, but she was willing to settle for less time than Doris formerly spent in looking after the little girls and in cleaning the house. After several discussions with her mother and father, Doris agreed that she would see that the two smallest children were dressed and ready for breakfast, as well as put them to bed after supper. She volunteered to pack the noon-day lunches she and her brother took to school, too, if she could be released from her Saturday morning duties. Participating in activities with her contemporaries that year was more important for Doris' development than taking extensive responsibilities for the three- and five-year-old sisters.

WHAT FORM SHALL RESPONSIBILITIES TAKE?

Parents cannot, of course, limit the eldest's tasks to certain hours or certain itemized performances at any age. To do so would defeat the attitude of being one's brother's keeper. Yet, both grown-ups and children lead such scheduled lives today that a degree of planning for definite times and stated duties usually makes for fewer arguments and for more freedom for both a mother and her deputy. If it is understood that the job of the eldest is seeing that one or two smaller ones arrive at the breakfast table, or the supper table, or get to bed, or get to school after having performed the necessary routines, then it can also be understood that certain hours are entirely free.

Mutual responsibility between members of the family does not stop or start at any precise moment. In addition to the specific, planned-for care and supervision, it can be made clear that each helps the other when that is necessary.

If there are several children in the family, and the oldest girl (for girls are more likely to be caught in this net than boys) is expected to look after the younger ones with no limits set either on her duties or her authority, the situation in the long run may benefit neither the eldest nor the younger ones.

The Crea family are an illustration of such a situation. Mrs. Crea was her husband's right hand in running the family's ranch. Since it was located in an isolated spot, the four girls and their brother had only one another's company on week-ends and after school. Lorna, the eldest, had looked after herself from the time she could walk. Soon after that, Lorna was supposed to keep a sister, one year younger, from wandering off limits, indoors and out. By the time she was five, she was helping this sister dress, seeing that the one next in line occasionally had her hands washed, and keeping an eye on a third who was creeping around with agility. At eight, Lorna was an accomplished nursemaid to her three sisters and a brother. She gave baths and settled arguments, repaired damaged toys and assuaged hurt feelings, administered band-aids and punishments. These duties gave expression to her affection for the smaller children. At the same time, as she reprimanded and criticized them, she was unloading resentment in a relatively harmless way.

Lorna rarely protested about the amount of time she spent looking after the other children. Like her mother, she seemed to think of herself as a person who was expected to carry heavy burdens and who was always hurrying to get done. Had there been other girls her own age nearby with whom she wanted to spend her time, she might have been a less willing supervisor.

The four younger children regarded Lorna as the font of all wisdom, and to a great extent their confidence in her was justified. She schooled her followers in the values of the world of childhood. Her approval or disapproval of their motives, as well as their actions, was usually well founded. So recently had she herself graduated from the stages they were passing through that she had a sharp eye for attempts to cover up a misdeed. When well-intentioned efforts were unsuccessful she was understanding and forgiving.

Mrs. Crea congratulated herself on having such a competent oldest daughter and left the younger children increasingly to Lorna's ministrations.

When Mrs. Crea's town-bred sister came for her annual visits, she would bemoan the fact that her own eldest son was far less inclined to take responsibilities than her niece. "But, of course, a girl growing up like this out in the country always is more responsible than a boy living in a two-family flat," would be the refrain of her recital.

An extensive piece of research on how children develop responsibility has demonstrated that this widely held notion is erroneous. Girls are not markedly more responsible than boys, nor does farm or ranch life make children more reliable in the matter of carrying out tasks than living in a city or a suburb.

Many eldest will tell you they like small children and have enjoyed taking care of younger brothers and sisters. Yet, in spite of the values present in the situation, can a girl or boy of seven or ten or fourteen stand so heady a dose of power as Lorna's? What does it do to the younger children to be mothered or fathered to so great an extent by a deputy?

To be a sister or a brother is a fairly complicated relationship. When too much of a parental role is superimposed on that relationship the benefits in the eldest's taking responsibilities begin to wane. Mothers and fathers need to keep their hands on the controls so that their judgment, not that of seven- or thirteen-year-olds gives family life its shape and texture.

Lorna's brother suffered from Lorna's authority. When he was three- and four- and five-years-old, he turned toward her the possessive love boys usually give their mothers during those years. A mother does not always find it easy to let her boy grow away from her. To a child like Lorna, such devotion is so flattering and expedient that she seeks to perpetuate it. This brother did remain dependent on Lorna throughout his childhood and in later life. When he grew up he could not marry until he found a girl of whom his sister approved. It is not surprising that nobody was quite good enough for him in her estimation.

As for Lorna, in addition to being far older than her years, she had too limited a range of relationships. She had learned to play only one part. As a result, she was the stern, all-wise mother to everyone with whom she came in contact, as she was growing up and later in life.

Lorna was so accustomed to thinking of herself as one who made sacrifices for others—an attitude she had caught from her mother—that when she won a scholarship to college she found the easy-going campus life distasteful. After one semester she turned her back on both the academic opportunities and the chance to take her place among her contemporaries, whom she dismissed as "silly." She stayed at home and continued to tell her brother and sisters what to do long after that became unnecessary.

Lorna never married. She made a home for her brother in the city where he settled, and took a position in an office. She was respected, but also feared by the younger women in her department to whom she gave unsolicited advice and whose lives she tried to run as she still attempted to rule her sisters.

THE FUTURE CANNOT BE SECURED

In looking ahead parents may worry about what will happen to their children in an unforeseeable future. For sentimental or for well-founded reasons, they may be anxious to ensure the eldest's continued care and concern for the younger ones. This is especially apt to be on a parent's mind if one of the children has a handicap or presents some difficulty, or if a mother or father has fears about his own life-expectancy.

To exact with death-bed solemnity a promise to look after a brother, keep the family together, or give a sister a home can do more harm than good. Nobody can know what circumstances will arise or how personalities will develop. The most any parent can do is to provide for his children in his own lifetime and create a home with an atmosphere of mutual support. An individual who grows up in such a family is not likely to turn his back on those who need him. Admonitions are either superfluous or, if carried out in the letter but not in the spirit, may blight the life of everyone involved.

If there is a member of the family who cannot look forward to taking care of himself, parents can plan for an arrangement which is clearly understood on all sides and which will not tie the eldest down to years of day-to-day responsibility. There can still be family solidarity and helpfulness, but there need not be tremendous sacrifice.

IS PAY FOR TAKING CARE OF YOUNGER ONES EVER JUSTIFIED?

A question that arises in many families centers around pay for the teen-ager who acts as baby sitter in his own home. A consideration of this point involves a clarification of duties versus allowances versus contributions to the life of the family.

Just because he is a member of the family, every child should make some contribution in time and effort toward the family's welfare and comfort. That includes looking after younger children as well as doing dishes or making beds.

Every child is entitled to a modest share in the family's resources, again, merely by virtue of the fact that he is a member of the group. Giving an allowance, not contingent on good behavior or performed tasks, is not instilling the false idea that one can get something for nothing. A child gets a new coat or a candy bar "for nothing." He even gets some toys, if his parents can afford them, without being forced to earn them. Yet if a small amount of cash is to be bestowed, some people are afraid a child's moral fiber will be weakened if it is given outright. An allowance does not interfere with learning the value of money. Getting paid for every small household job, including looking after brothers and sisters, can put an unfortunate price tag on jobs which might better be done in the spirit of participation and giving of yourself. Children are likely to become hagglers and wheedlers if they believe nickels, dimes, and quarters are the answer to every problem, and if rewards and penalties are too often phrased in terms of money.

Yet the experience of earning money occasionally by their own efforts is good for twelve- or thirteen- or fourteen-year-olds. One of the ways adolescent boys and girls can earn an honest dollar is by baby sitting. Looking after younger brothers and sisters and earning money are not incompatible under some circumstances.

One important aspect of this earning plan is that the boy or girl whose services are being requested has the right to refuse. The very act of choosing to go to the basketball game instead of earning a sum of money or vice versa is an edifying experience. In so doing a young person discovers what money cannot buy. An evening spent cheering the team may be priceless for one. Another, who is building a hi-fi set or who wants the latest in sweaters, may prefer the financial gain. The payment offered is for services to be performed. It is not a bribe.

Complications may follow in the wake of paying one's eldest for looking after younger members of the family. "If you hire me to stay home, because you'd have to get one of my friends to stay here if I didn't, can I have the gang over and give them cokes and cake?"

One father drew the line at that request. He made it clear that if his daughter expected to be paid for staying home to look after her younger brothers, the same rules would hold as when she engaged herself to be a sitter in another home. She might invite one girl to keep her company, but staging a party on those evenings was not permissible.

Parents who have had few evenings out during the years when all their children were young have a right to more freedom when an eldest can take charge. Since these are the very years when junior high or high school boys and girls want to go to a movie or to a party on a week-end evening, some delicate compromising is called for.

WHAT IS "TOO MUCH RESPONSIBILITY"?

At what point do responsibilities become a burden and cease to be good for either the eldest or for those in her care? A possible measuring stick might be:

Does this boy or girl still have time and zest for activities with his own friends?

Are there still some interests he pursues that have no connection with the other children in the family? That is not to say that a brother or sister should be excluded from the eldest's pursuits, but that if a younger one is included it should be because the eldest really wants his cooperation on the undertaking.

Is this oldest child able to get along in situations in which he is not playing the part of boss, or little mother, or is not, in the eyes of the other or in his own eyes, in control?

Are the responsibilities toward the younger children usually carried out without undue protest or procrastination? When friction, and nothing but friction, is resulting on both sides, the burdens imposed may be too heavy.

Have the responsibilities been worked out with the consent and cooperation of the eldest, and with the assent of the younger children—if they are old enough to be consulted?

If an affirmative answer to most of these questions holds true for a family much of the time, the eldest is probably not being pushed too hard.

Careful investigation as well as popular opinion substantiate the belief that when sacrifices are made in a family, the eldest is preeminently the one who makes them. The eldest's responsibilities can be tailor-made and frequently reviewed, so that they will be rewarding to the younger children as well as to the eldest, for in that way mutual trust and interdependence between the children will be furthered.

CHAPTER VII

The Eldest in a Group

WHAT DOES THE GROUP STAND FOR?

A child who has not found his juniors overwhelming, who has been on the whole a willing and responsible leader at home, is likely to anticipate a pleasant relationship with children away from home. He is generally able to make good use of what he has learned about winning allies, taking turns, and standing up for his own rights.

At the other end of the scale stands the child who, as eldest, has continually felt pushed aside. He, or she, has struggled unsatisfactorily to win from the powers that be proof of his own lovableness and value. For those youngsters, a group of children becomes, perhaps unconsciously, a multiplication of brothers and sisters with whom he must vie for the favor of the leader, or teacher, or counselor. He brings with him and transfers to the children he meets in school or camp the competitiveness which has been developed or heightened by his position in the family.

In going forth to become a participant in activities with other children, the eldest leaves one or more brothers or sisters behind. This complicates the meaning of the group by adding to it whatever significance leaving home has for him. For the small child, nursery school may appear to be a place of banishment to which he is relegated while his more fortunate brother or sister takes over home and mother. During the years of middle childhood, and sometimes to three- and four- and five-year-olds, a group may spell escape from brothers and sisters. Both these conflicting implications are probably present in varying degrees. What the group stands for to a child will influence his behavior in nursery school, on through kindergarten and the grades, as well as in recreational supervised gatherings. A group can do more for a child if it is a supplement to, rather than a duplication of, home.

NURSERY SCHOOL MAY BE A HAVEN

One of the original purposes of bringing children of four or three or even two years of age together for a few hours of play, stories, and music, or for a longer session including lunch and a nap, was to give them the opportunity to live a part of the day with others their own age in a child-paced world. To the eldest, playing with contemporaries who can carry out his ideas and add ideas of their own is more stimulating to his powers of invention and more fun than trying to put his plans for playing airplane or superman, cowboy or house, across to younger children at home. Nursery schools serve a more fundamental purpose, now that children tend to be so close in age in the larger middle and upper class families. Companionship is not the eldest's crying need. The opportunity to play alone, occasionally, unmolested by toddlers to whom he must give in and who destroy what he creates, is essential.

Teachers in many nursery schools are aware of the need which the group can fill for the hard-pressed eldest child. The boy or girl whose greatest delight is to build with blocks by himself in a corner of the room, to play alone with doll and doll carriage, to pull a wagon without having a friend, or an enemy, sitting in it, is not regarded as unsociable. The one who wants to stay in the playroom when the others go outside is not immediately branded as seriously nonconformist by the sensitive teacher today.

A four-year-old sat in the sand box letting the sand run through his fingers, paying no attention to the children around him and saying softly to himself, "Peace, it's peace, it's peace." He was expressing a feeling common to many of those eldest children who are benefited by a respite from the company of their still smaller brothers and sisters even more than by joining in activities with others.

A child who at home is unable to settle down to play because he is constantly checking on his mother to make sure she is not paying more attention to the younger ones than he finds bearable may be able to lose himself in an undertaking at nursery school. He, too, may be one who enjoys playing by himself.

HOW MUCH INDIVIDUAL ATTENTION?

The question of elasticity of routines raises another point underlying the thinking of adults in charge of a number of children: Is it fair to do for one what cannot be done for all. To phrase this in the terms in which it crops up in daily life, "What if all the children wanted to stay inside when it was time to go outdoors or what if everyone wanted to sit on the teacher's lap at the same moment?"

The law of averages tends to save nursery school teachers or mothers in charge of cooperative play groups from such dilemmas. When it comes time to go outdoors, or to take any other step in the day's routine, most children, with tactful guidance, will not balk. An oft-repeated protest on the part of a small child may suggest a particular need on his part. Is he, for example, anxious about something that may happen? Is he a chronic protester? Is he testing the adult to see what she will do? If he is allowed to go his own way instead of following along with the group, does he play contentedly and constructively or does he merely retreat further into himself and do nothing?

The same troublesome behavior in different children may be caused by widely differing conditions, yet some first-aid measures may be helpful in any case. The teacher who has reason to believe timidity is at the root of resistance may find that reassurance in words or holding the child's hand makes him less hesitant about the alarming move. The one who is trying out the adult to see what she will do may respond best to good-natured firmness. In the case of the chronic resister, there may be a deeper difficulty which bears looking into.

NURSERY SCHOOL CAN HELP HIM COME INTO HIS OWN

An eldest may be timid and withdrawn because so much emphasis has been placed by his parents on being quiet, good, and not competing with younger brothers and sisters. His perfectly natural tendency to seek the limelight may have been repeatedly rebuked as showing off. Such a child is likely not to play wholeheartedly and imaginatively with other children or by himself.

For him, the group can be the means of discovering that adults do not always disapprove when you are noisy, or get dirty using paints, clay, sand, water, or even mud, as mothers on occasions do at home. Such a child may eventually find, through the less restrictive atmosphere of nursery school, acceptable ways of expressing his feelings and satisfactory ways of communicating with others. As his feelings begin to thaw out, he may for a time be excitable and easily provoked to wild, silly behavior. If the adults in charge can guide him toward desirable means of gaining attention, and see that he gets the recognition he needs, he will really profit from his experience with group life.

WHEN PERSONS ARE BETTER THAN THINGS

The major gain for some eldest children in a nursery group comes from the relationship to the teachers. One three-year-old, in the early days of her enrollment, repeatedly expressed her scorn for the toys and the equipment. "I got better at home," this young materialist declared. Because the babies had absorbed her mother's time and her father's attention, this girl had missed warm, satisfying relationships. She had come to rely instead on elaborate playthings and lollipops to make life worth while.

The nursery school teachers took every opportunity to point out, "It's nice that you have toys at home, but here we have teachers and other children who will be your friends." They made a special effort to give her affection and to hold her on their laps. The adults in the school tried to convey the feeling that she was an important person in the group.

When she would beg for candy, she would be told, "I don't think you are hungry for candy. I think you are hungry for a hug. It wouldn't be taking good care of you to give you candy right now."

"Taking good care of you" had become one of the watch words

of the adults in this nursery school. The children, some of whom had actually not had good care at home, seemed to find this phrase a reassuring basis for regulations. Gradually, this girl discovered that affectionate interest can be more gratifying than mere things. She was no longer puzzled at the teacher's response to her requests for candy. Instead she would of her own accord climb on a favorite teacher's lap when she felt lonely or momentarily insecure.

Here is another change in the purpose nursery school serves, especially for the eldest. Opportunities to use blocks, clay, paints, dolls, and dress-up materials have become less important than they formerly were. One reason for this shift in emphasis, it must be acknowledged, is that every toy shop offers items that once could be found only in the nursery school playroom. A sutbler and more compelling reason for the preeminent place relationships take in the good nursery school today for eldest children is that many of them have been shortchanged on leisurely, gratifying, adult companionship at home. Teachers who have time to listen, to laugh, to make suggestions, or just stand by with encouragement while fumbling efforts are made constitute the nursery school's great contribution to some eldest boys and girls.

ELDESTS AS LEADERS

Some eldest children are a distinct asset in the nursery group. One who is accustomed to mothering smaller sisters and brothers may enjoy showing the younger or less competent ones how to use the housekeeping equipment, the trains, or the jungle gym. He may take newcomers by the hand and introduce them to the customs of the playroom. One lively four-year-old would pause in her own spirited interpretation of the music, when the children were gathered around the piano, to draw a shy youngster into hopping like a rabbit or galloping like a pony. A boy whose innate qualities of leadership had been fostered at home initiated playing store, or converted a large cardboard carton into a seagoing ship. By giving other children parts to act, he stimulated their interest and often raised the level at which they played. This boy helped other children find a place in the group and a role to play.

THEY BRING THEIR WORRIES WITH THEM

A first child who has been getting along reasonably well in the group may show a sudden change when a younger brother or sister is born. Hitting and kicking may become his preferred method of communication. Smaller children are likely to be the targets of his wrath. The choice of victim is dictated not so much by discretion in selecting those who cannot retaliate as by a distaste for anything or anyone who suggests infancy.

The deterioration in control may be due to general uneasiness as well as impatience with those with whom he must share adult attention in any setting. Teachers can help these distressed boys and girls by seeing that they receive an extra measure of adult affection. They can be watched carefully so that when a situation is taxing their endurance, they can be directed into another activity before they reach the hitting point.

Legitimate outlets for aggressive acts such as hammering nails into wood, pounding a chunk of clay, assaulting a stuffed and weighted figure which rolls with the punches, throwing or kicking a large, bouncing ball may be serviceable devices for draining off anger.

Temporary isolation for a child who is consumed with fury may sometimes be in order. The emphasis can be on staying alone "until you feel better" or "until you can come back and ask for what you want."

Experiences in the group can help the eldest child as he tries to manage his conflicting feelings. One of a teacher's most valuable allies in nursery school, kindergarten, and in the primary grades is "show and tell"—that period in the day when children are asked to stand up and talk about events that are of vital importance to them.

A teacher's casual response to comments that reveal an unspoken anxiety about a change in status following the arrival of a new baby can dispel some of an eldest's doubts and reassure him that he is not a second-class member of his family. Such remarks can also ease worries not only for the child who announced the news, but for others who are in a similar predicament.

An occasional story or song which highlights the fact that it is good to be first in the family can give an eldest child added stature. Public recognition of prestige often carries more weight than what is said at home. These stories, too, show youngsters how someone in a position similar to their own has worked out difficulties. As they take on the feelings of the characters in the story, they tend to become less guilty about their own resentment, especially if the tale does not depict superhuman perfection. Their own latent fondness for a younger brother or sister is often reinforced by stories expressing an older brother or sister's affection for the baby.

One nursery school teacher made up a game in which pictures and conversation were both used to explain about mother hens who have room under their wings for all their chickens. When children gathered around her for music or a story she would stretch out her arms to include all their number and say "Here is the mother hen who has room under her wings for all her chickens." The children would laugh contentedly and draw closer. Occasionally she would add, "Your mother has room for all her chickens under her wings too." This device was helpful to those eldests who were visibly disturbed by the addition of a new child to the nursery school.

Honoring the boy or girl who reports a new baby at home or some signal achievement of a younger brother or sister by giving him a coveted responsibility or giving him a special privilege demonstrates the pleasing fact that being the eldest has some rewards. This device is as useful with five-, six- or seven-year-olds as with three- and four-year-olds.

TWO OF A KIND MAKE A FULL HOUSE

Brothers and sisters so close in age that two or even three are in the same nursery group may create a problem for the eldest. Three- or -four-year-olds will often talk constantly of the younger ones at home. When they climb high on the jungle gym or shoot swiftly down the slide, they announce, "My sister couldn't do that." Easter baskets, Christmas tree decorations, and paintings are taken home to show the baby because "he wouldn't know how to do anything this hard."

Nursery school pupils are usually eager to have smaller brothers, or sisters, take part in their school activities.

When that day comes, however, it may not be as happy a situation as the elder anticipated. This was the case with Ronnie. At four he was one of the senior group at school. After his sister, Mimi, fourteen months his junior, joined the three-year-old group, Ronnie spent most of his time standing at the door between the two playrooms watching Mimi. When he saw Miss English, his favorite teacher when he had been with the three's, speak to or do anything for Mimi, his face would pucker up, his fists would be clenched, and he would lash out wildly at any child who happened to be near him. He had looked forward with such feverish excitement to his sister's being at school that for the first few days the teachers considered his interest in her a quite natural fraternal protectiveness. Probably that did enter into his feelings, but as his concern over what Mimi was doing mounted rather than decreased in the following weeks the teachers decided he was somewhat troubled.

Mimi, already well established, had no need to seek out her brother as younger children so often do. At this nursery school four-year-olds stayed for mid-day meal and nap, a practice Ronnie had concurred in without question. Now, he would cling to his mother when she came to take Mimi home and insist that either he would go home with her or Mimi must stay at school, too. In vain did his teacher talk about what he would be missing if he left before the story and lunch. Stressing that having lunch at school was the privilege of big boys failed to convince him also. Mimi's remaining at school was out of the question, not only because it was against policy, but also because she was thoroughly tired and needed to be quiet at home.

In a conference with the head teacher Ronnie's mother related that her daughter had seen a picture in a magazine which she declared was her Miss English. Ronnie grew angry, grabbed the magazine, and tore it up. This account gave the teacher a new approach. She explained to his mother that she proposed to take a firm stand about Ronnie's staying for lunch, not to show him that he couldn't have everything he wanted, but to help him discover that Mimi's gain was not necessarily his loss. To that end she would arrange to have Miss English ask him to sit with her at lunch and spend extra time with him after Mimi went home.

The next day when Miss English joined the four-year-olds for lunch, she put her arm around Ronnie and said, "Let's you and me eat together today." Ronnie loked dubious. "Mimi, too?," he asked. Miss English explained that Mimi was going home as all the three-year-olds did. Ronnie stayed without too much protest that day and with decreasing reluctance thereafter. Sitting next to his favorite and having her settle him in his cot for his nap seemed to make it worth letting his sister have their mother for herself.

At home when arguments arose as to whom Miss English belonged to, and whom she liked best, the mother, following the head teacher's recommendations, would say, "She's Mimi's Miss English in the morning, and she's your Miss English at noon, and do you know, when I go to a coffee party at your school, she's my Miss English too. She likes us all, and we like her." Ronnie insisted dourly that he wanted to be liked best, but his mother let the matter rest there.

Ronnie never seemed quite as free at nursery school as he had been before his sister came. Too often he had an eye on her to see whether she was getting more than her share of attention. Other things being equal, life might have been easier for the boy had his sister's entrance in school been delayed another season until he had gone on to kindergarten, for the school had been the one place where he had not had to compete with her. Children cannot escape completely from competitive situations, but sometimes they need a temporary refuge from them.

One partial solution which some nursery schools have found useful in such a situation is to let the younger child, or children, come to school three days a week while the eldest is on the regular Monday to Friday schedule. Another plan that has worked well when the presence of younger members of the family have an unfavorable effect on the eldest is to arrange a slightly different program for the oldest and his particular friends. Putting members of the same family in different groups with different teachers, if the nursery school staff is large enough to permit doing so, also avoids reproducing the rivalries of home. Above all, treating the children as distinct individuals and remembering the preferences and at least the names and the clothes of each makes the lot of both the younger and the older more agreeable.

These three special gains can accrue to the eldest in a well-managed nursery school: He can have the companionship of children who are his equals or superiors in inventiveness. He can have some chance to play by himself and pursue his own concerns even in the midst of other children without having them be as much in his way as brothers and sisters are at home. Finally, he can have a relationship with friendly adults which may fill in some of the gaps in his emotional life at home and extend the circle of those to whom he feels he can turn for help.

FEELINGS COME TO GRADE SCHOOL, TOO

The ways in which the group is helping, or sometimes hindering, development usually appears more clearly in eldest children below grade-school age. Because both the program and the child are more flexible in groups of three-, four- or five-year-olds, it is possible for teachers to create situations that will provide for individual needs more readily than can be done in elementary classrooms.

The leadership which distinguishes some eldest children in their early days may continue through the grades. One second grader, accustomed to taking the lead at home, instigated and helped organize a school safety patrol. Another eldest, in fourth grade, took charge when the teacher was called away from the classroom and kept the group working busily. Those who have found satisfaction in their responsibilities at home look for responsibilities to assume at school. Of such stuff are frequently made monitors and chairmen, captains and members of the school council, not to mention honor students.

Those who are the eldest at home are not invariably leaders, nor do they always have a head start on leadership in grade school. Those who have been younger ones in a family and who have become wise in the ways of childhood by copying older brothers and sisters often have an advantage over eldests who must be the pathfinders in their own families.

Just because a boy or girl has carried great responsibility at home does not guarantee that he or she will take on leadership in school. Bernice was a sixth-grade girl who shouldered a heavy load at home as the first in a family of five. Her mother was usually ailing and her father was far from dependable. Bernice cooked, looked after her mother, and cared for the four younger children. She saw to it that her father arose and left for work on time. She was at once the hub of the family and its driving force. At school she withdrew rather sullenly from contact with other children, probably out of sheer fatigue and anxiety. Responsible leadership to this twelve-year-old had been for several years so demanding that she had no desire to have any of it in school. She seldom expressed an opinion. Her work was mediocre. Being a nonentity in the classroom seemed to be a saving relief from the taxing role she was forced into at home.

In sharp contrast to such a girl who seems to be lost in the group is the child who is impelled to seek the limelight constantly. Most teachers are familiar with the boy or girl whose work is satisfactory but who needs to be repeatedly reassured of the fact. If the teacher praises another child, such a youngster becomes downcast. Such children are often the eldest in their own families and for that reason tend to be threatened when it appears that anyone will outdo or overtake them. They may be seeking the favor of the teacher as they have sought the favor of their mothers and fathers. They have so often felt pushed aside that when anything that seems to be a rebuff comes their way, they feel wounded out of all proportion to the actual facts in the case.

Since their inability to let anyone else have a place in the sun can become a serious handicap to them, both teachers and parents can try to provide the emotional vitamins they need to cure their undernourished feelings. These boys and girls are not gluttons for recognition, rather they are starved for it. The emotional diet that usually improves their condition is the one that has been recommended before. Encouragement, opportunities to succeed, and to be acclaimed as a worth while, loved individual, as well as to have a share of his mother's and father's time, and if possible, a teacher's, are a tonic, but not a specific, for these children. Less stress on competition both at home and in school usually benefits them too.

Another facet of this same insecurity is a consuming avidity for popularity. The girl who spends the first three weeks of the school year trying to get into a club four other girls have formed, and then spends the next three weeks breaking it up because "it's no good anyway," is a pathetic figure. She wants to be in everything not because she enjoys the companionship or the activity, but because she is mortally afraid of being left out. A compelling drive to be popular is often an effort to find somewhere that preeminent position and exclusive affection the eldest feels he or she has been denied at home. Sometimes the intensely competitive girl or boy who wants to be included in everything and to be first in every undertaking contributes to the group by sparking new enterprises. He or she may have great energy and imagination. If teachers can help such a child find satisfaction in an activity for its own sake, not just because it brings recognition, or in the company of classmates who become friends and not merely stepping stones, they will be setting him on the way toward a happier, more useful life. As he becomes more self-sufficient, he will not be impelled to demand attention in so many ways.

If the classroom atmosphere is not overcompetitive, if more emphasis is placed on the quality of a piece of work or of a friendship and less on being part of every venture, this kind of child may be less intensely concerned about popularity. If the classroom situation is handled well, an overcompetitive eldest may gain more faith in himself and more tolerance for the success of others, from his contacts with the group.

In crowded classrooms it is not easy to allow individual differences a chance to enrich the group. Yet, if a teacher can help each child make his unique contribution and value it because it is unique, she is giving her students the courage to be themselves. In this day that is no small matter. The child who can find satisfactions in being part of a group and still retain his individuality is likely to be less jealous, less fiercely and unwholesomely competitive than one who feels others have a monopoly on the desirable traits and therefore look down on him.

One talented fifth-grade teacher succeeded in making almost every one of the thirty or thirty-five children in her classes feel specially valued. She played up the abilities of each by encouraging the children to bring their interests into the classroom. The bulletin board and window sills in her room were covered with exhibits the children had brought to school. Collections of timetables and china dogs, seashells and stamps, even bottle tops and matchbook covers were all grist to her mill. Each child was invited to talk for a few minutes about his collection or demonstrate some angle of his hobby. Where this teacher went beyond the call of duty was in remembering each child's interest. During the year she found opportunities to ask how it was progressing, to suggest a book to look for or a line of inquiry to pursue. If it was at all possible to tie a child's hobby into the subject matter of social studies, literature or even arithmetic, she would do so. Of course all the children benefited by this technique, but those who needed particular reassurance because of emotional scars left over from earlier experiences were especially strengthened.

FEELINGS INTERFERE WITH LEARNING

Some children with good intelligence do not learn to read or cannot grasp the elementary facts about numbers, no matter how good the teaching they receive. As a result, they dislike school and cannot take their place in the group. Eventually, they become troublemakers.

The accusation frequently is that they do not try or that they cannot concentrate. What prevents a child from trying to learn? Learning requires a bold effort. Happy, healthy children have a lively curiosity and usually enjoy attacking a problem. If they continually resist learning there is a deeper reason. That reason in an eldest often is that he has been so impressed with the wrongness of competing, showing off, or being curious that unconsciously he feels it is safer to retreat than to put himself forward in any way. Approval, he believes, can only come from being self-effacing, and not learning is a kind of self-effacement.

If tests of readiness and ability indicate there is no mental deficiency; if vision, hearing, and general health are good, then the possibility that unconscious fears are at the root of the trouble should be explored. Learning disabilities rarely yield to home remedies, but they do diminish—sometimes with surprising rapidity—if a child can have the help of a professional person skilled in handling children's emotional problems. Parents and teachers tend to postpone seeking such help in the hope that a sudden change for the better will occur or that drill and practice will provide a solution. Repeated failure makes matters worse for the child.

Prompt help is worth every effort that may be involved in securing it. School counselors, family service associations, mental health societies, the family's doctor or the school's, can often suggest the clinic or professional person who may be of help. Such assistance while a boy or girl is in the early grades may make the difference between an individual's being effective or ineffective not only in school but throughout his life.

GROWING THROUGH DISCUSSION

The eldest and his problems may come more directly into classroom discussion in junior high and high school, or even in the intermediate grades. Some teachers have found that reading a story to the class in which a conflict between brothers and sisters or children and parents is high-lighted, and then allowing the children to talk it over, brings out feelings which have been troubling a child. Often, too, through the various points of view expressed by the children, new ideas may take root and increased understanding may blossom. A classroom or an informal organized group can provide a good setting for expressing feelings. While the teacher or leader and the children know one another, they are not as embroiled with one another as the children in a family are likely to be.

Material for such discussion is to be found in abundance. The Center for Intergroup Education at the University of Chicago collected a diversified bibliography, *Reading Ladders for Human Relations* (Wash., American Council on Education, 1948). *With Focus on Human Relations* by Deborah Elkins and Hilda Taba, Wash. American Council on Education, 1950) tells the story of how human relations material, including the relationship of children in the family, was used in a classroom. *How Brothers and Sisters Get Along Together* by Marie Louise Kreidl (published by the Department of Guidance and Secondary School Curriculum of the Schools of the City of South Bend, Indiana, 1950) sets forth a stimulating program.

Other books for children in which the eldest figures prominently are to be found in Appendix V of this book. *The Chicago Schools Journal*, March-April Supplement, 1950, contains a useful bibliography in "Developmental Values Through Library Books," by Effie La Plante and Thelma O'Donnell. *Character Formation through Books: A Bibliography* (Wash., Catholic University of America Press, 1952), compiled by Clara J. Kircher, is also helpful.

In addition, these short stories and selections are excellent points of departure for discussion in junior high school classes:

Nan Gilbert, "Little Susie's Upper Cut," *Adventures for Readers,* Book I, N. Y., Harcourt, Brace, 1947. (Mercury Ed.)

Zachary Gold, "I Got A Name," *Saturday Evening Post Stories of 1938-42*, Boston, Little Brown, 1942.

Zachary Gold, "The Top of the Mountain," *Teen-Age Companion*, N. Y., Lantern Press, 1946. (Also in *Saturday Evening Post Stories of 1942-45*, N. Y., Random House, 1945.)

George Loveridge, "Martha," *Saturday Evening Post Stories,* *1942-45,* N. Y., Random House, 1945.

Irwin Shaw, "Strawberry Ice Cream Soda," *Here We Are, Stories from Scholastic Magazine,* N. Y., Dodd, Mead, 1941. (Also in *Short Story Craft,* N. Y., Macmillan, 1949.)

Val Teal, "A Date for Dorothy," *The Years Between,* Chicago, Scott, Foresman, 1953.

Since the books suggested in these lists are the very ones which librarians, teachers, and parents, not to mention the children themselves, agree are top literary fare, such reading and discussion may appropriately find a place in the hours devoted to literature in a classroom.

Those who claim that schools have strayed from their primary purpose of teaching content have no cause to complain about these discussions of human conduct based on literature. Actually, the child who catches the feelings of the characters in a story and lives through that character's experiences is learning far more about the book under consideration than one who merely identifies figures of speech.

Some teachers have provoked excellent discussion by stopping the reading just before the story's climax, when the characters are deeply involved in conflict, to ask the group, "What do you think should happen now?" or "What would you do if you were in that situation?" or "Why do you think the sister acted that way?" Without realizing it, the children are working out some of their own problems in attempting to solve the dilemmas of the characters in the story.

Another useful device in increasing understanding of themselves and other members of the family is to act out incidents. The episode that comes out in discussion or an incident portrayed in the story may lend itself to dramatization. As each child throws himself into his part he experiences the feelings of the character he is portraying. A discussion of how role-playing may be used in the classroom can be found in *Helping Children With Specific Needs,* Teachers' Guidance Handbook, Elementary School Edition. Vol. II, 1956, and Secondary School Edition, Vol. II, 1957,

Science Research Associates, Chicago.

Personalities are not remade nor are problems of five or ten years standing neatly solved in this way. Still, children do discover they are not alone in the situation they face or in the conflicting feelings they experience.

THE SOLITARY ELDEST

When a child stands apart from the group in nursery school or kindergarten, parents and teachers are ready to believe that he will outgrow this tendency and become more interested in companionship. Often, that is exactly what happens, if the adults in his life give him some assistance. When a grade-school child consistently avoids joint projects, and does not seem to enjoy being part of a group, parents and teachers in the United States of America are concerned. The cartoon showing the irate father reading the report card of a very small boy, captioned "Now you get in there and integrate with the group, see?" hits close to the mark for us. In other places in the world, for example in France, making friends and being a good member of a group is far from the primary task of a boy or girl. In the United States our entire culture stresses the need for taking one's place in whatever group one finds oneself, and rewards those who perform satisfactorily as members of a team.

A child who has turned to the adults rather than to the other children in the family for most of his pleasant relationships may remain on the fringe of the group. Several causes may contribute to this state of affairs. On the basis of his past experience, he may find adult company more agreeable. He may have been exposed to large doses of grown-up conversation at home and be somewhat bored with childish things. Such a child may make his contribution to the classroom through his wider background of general information which can expand the horizons of the other children. As his value to the group as the one who knows about stars, or plants, or automobiles, or maps is recognized, his classmates may spontaneously accord him the recognition he often secretly craves.

In order to help the eldest who is not sociable teachers and parents need to be clear about their goals. Must everyone have the team spirit? Is there a place for the boy or girl who enjoys solitary pursuits? Many a creative, self-sufficient individual who likes to be alone because he finds pleasure in reading, drawing, or tinkering with machinery, can lead a full life. He does not need to be made to feel there is something wrong with him because he is less avid for company and cooperative activities than other children. If he has a few friends and occasionally takes part in group life, his parents and teachers may be satisfied and let him go his own way.

The boy or girl who avoids others and shuns taking part in a group and who is also steadily apathetic, furtive, and antagonistic presents an entirely different picture. He may need the help of a professional person qualified to deal with deeper problems, not because he wants to walk by himself, but because he is walking by himself into dangerous territory.

Whether a child's position as the eldest in the family tends to make him a person who is more or who is less acceptable to other children has been studied from many angles. Being the eldest does not invariably predispose an individual to being sociable, though one study has shown eldests to rate high in acceptability. The results of two different studies suggest that those children who are best liked come from smaller families and do not have brothers or sisters extremely close in age.

AFFECTION CAN BE DILUTED

When the eldest goes to a day camp or a summer camp where he lives for several weeks he encounters a number of adults who as counselors become important to him. Instead of the intensity of a child's relation with a mother and father, his devotion becomes diluted among the adults in the camp. This experience may give him evidence that exclusive possession of one adult is not the sole road to satisfaction. That is a lesson the eldest needs to learn.

Somewhat the same benefit may be derived from those family camps with varied but definitely scheduled activities, some planned for those of approximately the same age, and some for groups with similar interests, regardless of age. Here a school-age child has a chance to work and play with adults in a relationship different from what he has known with either parents or teachers.

THE GROUP OFFERS A NEW ROLE

In a summer camp an eldest boy or girl can have a vacation from himself and play a different part from the one he plays at home. For one twelve-year-old boy, being with a slightly older age group turned out well. He had three younger sisters at home. He had been pushed into the role of protector—the strong, but forbearing, and tolerant one. He also was exposed to an inordinate amount of feminine conversation. He was constantly admonished not to be rude or rough, and to observe the rule of ladies first with his sisters who took full advantage of their immunity. To spend a month in the company of men and boys, particularly older boys, was a great relief and a refreshing experience for him.

Some children who have been the eldest in their own families echo the sentiments of one fourteen-year-old girl. When asked if she wanted to assist the counselors on a hike with the ten-year-olds, she exclaimed, "Spend the whole day with those brats? Who calls that a vacation?"

Some eldests who have enjoyed being maternal or protective to younger brothers and sisters will continue to play that part at camp or in a similar setting. Still, being protective to those who are not members of the family offers a welcome change. These young people are eager to become junior counselors, counselors in training, or assistant leaders, and often become outstanding in such positions.

Life in a well-run camp can be sufficiently leisurely so that counselors can know the girls and boys in their charge well. There can be time to find out what interests each, what he likes in others and in himself. For some eldests, to feel singled out by an admired adult, to be praised when something has been well done, or to be encouraged if a beginning has been made is an experience which heightens their own self-respect. Because these first-borns have been thrown on their own to a great extent, they feel that their accomplishments have gone unnoticed. Not so much the group, itself, as the contact with the adult leader exerts the beneficial influence.

Similar benefits may come to the eldest in boys' clubs, Scout troops, or other organizations. A ten-year-old girl in a community center club said to the leader, "What I like here is that I'm not always the one who has to think things up. At home, my mother's always saying, 'Can't you find something for the little ones to do?' She's always telling them to ask me to fix something or show them how something works. I honestly get sick of my own ideas." This girl was anything but a leader in the club, yet she made a real contribution by being an enthusiastic member.

The girl in this same club who was most resourceful in making plans and the first to volunteer for any task involving responsibility was also the eldest in her family. She was happy when she could be the one who found a way. An adult working with a group needs to be prepared to find such opposite responses from children who have occupied similar positions in their own families. Each is gaining from her experience in the group in her own way.

THE GROUPS HE CHOOSES IN LATER LIFE

An eldest's choice of a group and his behavior in it in adulthood may be rooted in a long forgotten experience with a younger brother or sister. This is illustrated in *Arrival and Departure*, by Arthur Koestler (N. Y., Macmillan, 1943). The central character, Peter Slavek, had endured torture and actually sought martyrdom out of what he believed was loyalty to the Cause to which he had given his allegiance. Through Sonia, the psychoanalyst, he discovers that the part he had played and the suffering he had undergone was not rational devotion in line with what circumstances demanded. His actions toward the Cause and those allied with it had unconsciously been influenced by his guilt over a grisly accident to his younger brother twenty years ago. The accident had not been his fault, but so intense had been his resentment against this brother that his unconscious feeling was "my evil wishes brought this about." In adulthood he had continuously sought punishment for his imagined crime. Anxiety about expiating his guilt had impelled him to sacrifice everything, including life itself.

Not many persons are driven to such extremes, still one of the forces that attracts an individual to a particular group often is that he has transferred to it feelings he once had about a brother or sister. Perhaps the attraction lies in the fact that the groups' methods give him a chance to work out in an acceptable disguise feelings about other children in the family. An individual who deeply resented the fact that the younger children had privileges he had been denied but who feared to express his feelings will frequently, years later, find himself at home in a group dedicated to persecuting those of a certain race, or faith, or economic class.

THE ELDEST NEEDS THE GROUP AND GROUPS NEED THE ELDEST ONES

From nursery school days on through high school, in formal or informal groups, eldest children play a variety of parts and derive a variety of benefits. Leadership and responsibility come naturally and are congenial to some of them. Others may find relaxation in avoiding it. All children profit by a warm and friendly relationship with adults outside the family, but the eldest may have a special need for adult recognition.

Some eldests turn toward the adults in the group and do not join eagerly in undertakings with other children. For an eldest the group offers the opportunity to step out of his usual role and become the younger one.

Whether a group provides gratifying sociability or an escape from the burdens he feels he carries as eldest, teachers, leaders, and counselors can help a first-born child make his contribution to and benefit from the group. If adults understand the strains and the satisfactions the first-born has experienced in his own family, they are better able to provide the kind of atmosphere that will help him grow into his best self.

CHAPTER VIII

Special Situations

The eldest in a family that includes an adopted child or twins has a special slant on life. The one parent family, a step-parent, or the household with three generations presents the first-born with a set of conditions different from those he would meet in the more usual arrangement. The pseudo-eldest, whose parents lost a child before this one was born, encounters unique problems, while the death of a younger brother or sister puts the older in a situation of still another kind. How can adults help the boy or girl who because of any of these family patterns has hazards to surmount?

There is no stereotype for any of these situations. The personalities of the individuals involved, their previous experiences, their interaction with one another, the eldest's phase of development at the moment of crisis, and to a lesser degree external circumstances shape the way conditions will be met. This, in turn, determines whether the development of the eldest will be helped or hampered. Being aware of some frequently observed responses can assist adults in recognizing danger signals, and accepting behavior which while inconvenient is still fostering a child's mastery of his problems.

Under any of these conditions a child especially needs the feeling that there is one adult in his life who loves him whether he is good or bad and who will stand by him. It is reassuring to remember, too, that if parents can accept a state of affairs without undue guilt or anxiety, children are better able to cope with conditions.

WHEN THE ELDEST IS ADOPTED

Parents who have decided to adopt a child usually have good reasons for wanting to do so and have given the matter thoughtful consideration. In addition to their conscious, rational motives, there are usually unconscious ones which shape their attitudes toward themselves as parents and toward the child they take into their home.

If, then, after their adopted son or daughter has come to live with them, the mother becomes pregnant, their feelings may be confused. Two children may be an embarrassment of riches, especially if close in age. Two or later more to provide for may create an unforeseen economic problem. Some parents feel guilty about the situation and fear they will not be able to give the adopted child his due. Others may worry lest the adopted one's presence interfere with the birthright of their own child. Even so superficial a matter, for example, as having named the adopted one after a beloved member of the family may cause them to wonder if they have been giving away what should rightfully belong to their own son or daughter.

Parents with several children of their own often have similar misgivings when another child is to be born into the family, especially if, as is so often the case with a post-adoptive baby, it was not specifically included in the parents' plans for the future. Like most emotions of the parents of adopted and natural children, these feelings differ in degree rather than in kind from the feelings of parents who have only their own children.

So much emphasis has been placed on letting a child know, as soon as he can understand, that he was chosen that it will be assumed this procedure is generally followed. The question of adoption has been discussed in *Adoption and After,* (N. Y., Harper, 1955) by Louise Raymond, and *The Adopted Family,* (N. Y., Crown, 1951) Book I, by Florence Rondell and Ruth Michaels, which are among the excellent books on the subject parents will want to read.

Parents who are prepared for the inevitable resentment when

the baby arrives, or when it gets in the elder one's way, and for rivalry as he grows up will be less likely to attribute every difficulty to the fact that the older is adopted.

Some parents stress so heavily that the first child was selected because "we looked until we found what we wanted, and that was you," that the child born into the family feels his state is less desirable. That feeling is heightened when the older one puts forth as incontrovertible evidence of his superiority the fact that he was chosen. There is such a thing as being adoption-proud. In moderation, it may serve a purpose, but when it is overdone, like any other form of snobbery, it probably covers doubts about one's own worth.

A mother who had two adopted children and one natural child had been troubled by the arguments among the children as to which method of entering the family made one more valued. One day when the debate was particularly acrimonious, she called the children to her. She was sitting in a room that had three exits. She told each child to sit down and then directed each to leave the room by a different door and wait until he was called. One at a time she summoned them from the several doors. Then she said, "Now we're all together, aren't we? You each came in by a different door, didn't you? You see, how you got here doesn't make any difference now that we are together."

This symbolic dramatization pleased the children so greatly that the youngest, who was then five, wanted it repeated on various occasions and it became a family ceremony. It did not put an end to the bickering, but it did seem to reduce the heatedness of that controversy. Disputes which revolve around the relative merits of adoption versus blood relationship are of the same significance as the point of departure of other quarrels children have. It makes one more convenient hook on which to hang an argument, but as in other squabbles, the core is a struggle for status and for the favor and possession of the parents.

"MY OWN MOTHER WOULD HAVE BEEN BETTER"

The most wounding phrase to many adoptive parents, particularly if they have a child of their own as well, is "My own mother would have understood," or "My own father would never treat me this way." In fact, a wily pre-adolescent or adolescent with a theatrical flair may use this argument because he knows it distresses his parents and makes it easier for him to get what he wants.

As armor against this poison arrow, mothers and fathers can realize that frequently a child born into a family will imagine he is adopted and that somewhere in the world are his own parents who would deny him nothing. Such children often ask whether they are adopted, or insist they are, even when their parents assure them such is not the case. One six-year-old who inquired whether he was adopted seemed disappointed when told he was not. "Too bad," he remarked, "I thought maybe I had a better mother."

For an adopted child who sees his present mother caring for another boy or girl, it is but a short step to "My own mother would not have given her love to another," or "She isn't my own mother. How can she love me now?"

When this occurs, parents may momentarily regret that they have told this child he is adopted. His protest arises not because he knows of the adoption but because he is having the universal struggle to share a parent or accept a restriction. It is not easier in the long run to keep the knowledge that he is adopted from a child.

THE ADOPTED ONE MAY BE TREATED MORE LENIENTLY

If his own child reminds him of a member of the family he dislikes, a parent may find himself more comfortable with the one who has been adopted. If a parent thinks he sees in his own son or daughter certain weaknesses which have plagued him throughout his life, he may be unjustifiably irritable in dealing with that child. Parents find it harder to excuse a child of their own if his behavior is not all they hoped for, since he is really an extension of themselves. The adopted one may be treated more casually and consequently feel less pushed.

THE ADOPTED YOUNGER BROTHER OR SISTER

If parents have a child of their own and then adopt another, the older one goes through the same emotions he would have if a baby were born into the family plus the question in his mind about his own adequacy, since his parents, he believed, were not willing to risk having a baby of their own again.

If the parents of an only child of six or seven years adopt a boy or girl a year or two younger with the idea of providing a companion for the first-born, they may be disappointed if the children do not prove congenial. Much as he may appear to want a brother or sister, the elder's feelings will be mixed when his parents actually select one and bring him home to live. The cross currents of affection and resentment that characterize relations of children in the family are present here, too, and a full-blown personality is usually harder to accept than a baby.

Books for children in which an adopted child figures help the eldest as he works out his problems in relation to his own adoption or to the adopted brother or sister. Children under the age of six will enjoy: *The Chosen Baby*, by Valentina Wasson (Phil., Lippincott, 1950); *The Family That Grew*, by Florence Rondell and Ruth Michaels (N. Y., Crown, 1954). For children from six to eight years of age: *Here's a Penny*, by Carolyn Haywood (N. Y., Harcourt, Brace, 1944); *Penny and Pete,* by Carolyn Haywood (N. Y., Harcourt, Brace, 1944); *The Adopted Family*, Book II, by Florence Rondell and Ruth Michaels (N. Y., Crown, 1951). Highschool boys and girls will enjoy *Room for One More,* by Anna Perrot Rose (Boston, Houghton Mifflin, 1950).

MINORITY RIGHTS

When twins are the eldest in a family, they are usually in a happy position, even though their mother may be under great pressure. Since they have each other, many of the experiences which give being the eldest its special significance are never theirs. Parents of twins will find a practical approach to their perplexities in *The Care and Feeding of Twins,* by Phyllis Graham

(N.Y., Harper, 1955), and a discussion of the psychological aspects of their relationship in *Twins* by Dorothy Burlingham (N.Y., International Universities Press, 1952).

The eldest who is followed by twins in the family is faced with acute competition. He is confronted with much more than two individuals. The two plus their twinship are a formidable array, for twins are often, as Dorothy Burlingham has pointed out, a gang in miniature. Because of their closeness and their ability to communicate with each other almost wordlessly, the singleton eldest is at a disadvantage. He has no one with whom he can make common cause. His parents are a couple, and so are the twins. The adults in the family, bemused by the double miracle the twins present, may fail him. Because twins are always the center of attraction no matter how parents try to equalize matters, other people may pay more attention to them than to the eldest.

In *The Fountain Overflows* (N. Y., Viking, 1956) Rebecca West has portrayed the plight of an eldest girl with twin sisters. This is not the chief theme of the book, yet it does become the climax. Cordelia, the eldest, prettier than her twin sisters, but less gifted musically, and conventional to the point of stuffiness in an eccentric family has striven to become a concert violinist. When she learns she has no talent, she collapses and cries in despair, "If I am not to be a famous violinist, how am I ever to get away from you all?"

Cordelia's isolation from her warm, dynamic family is not due merely to her being, as they claim, stupid musically, but to the fact that the twins together are such a congenial and forceful unit. They could share a bed, an opinion, or a piano with comfort, but Cordelia is an outsider. Her tragedy was not that she could not get on well with her sisters, but that they could get along so nicely without her.

Parents who are bringing up a singleton eldest and twins can be alert to the rights and needs of the minority as the twins grow out of babyhood and routines and arrangements no longer need to revolve around them.

A warm relationship with an adult outside the immediate family may help an eldest under these circumstances. If a grandparent, aunt or uncle or neighbor becomes his champion, he may feel there is someone with whom he comes first and whom he is not required to share with the twins.

Parents can make a special effort to show their interest in the affairs of the eldest by being on hand when he takes part in a play, or a recital, or when they are asked to turn up at school in his behalf. It is easy to become so engulfed by the duplicate demands that the eldest's are dwarfed in importance.

If the twins are treated more as separate individuals and less as a unit, and their individuality stressed more than their similarity, the eldest has a less formidable situation to contend with. If the twins are identical rather than fraternal, this is harder to do, for they have an almost eerie oneness. Relationships can be improved all around when the twins are addressed by their own names and not referred to as "the twins."

If there is as much as five or six years difference in age between the first child and the twins, the eldest may take more than the usual pride in caring for them. Since everyone stops to comment on twins, he who is in charge of them basks in reflected glory. Yet reflected glory should not be the eldest's only portion, as it was in the case of a girl with twin brothers five years younger. She was so willing to be their faithful servitor that she was in danger of losing any individuality of her own.

THE ELDEST IN A ONE-PARENT FAMILY

The great hazard for the eldest who has been deprived of a parent by death or divorce is that the burden of taking that place will fall on him, eventually, if not immediately particularly if he is of the opposite sex from the parent with whom he lives. His own identification with the father or mother prompts him to do what he thinks the absent one would have done. The remaining parent may consciously or unconsciously assign him that role, by leaning heavily on him. Outsiders in a well-meant effort to inspire him and invoke his cooperation often say, "You'll take your father's place," or to a daughter, "You will be the mother now."

Even in temporary absences of a parent, the oldest boy who is told, "You must be the man of the family" frequently shows by his behavior how confusing a role this command puts on him. As a life-time obligation it is certainly unfortunate.

Most children try to behave in the courageous, sensible, grown-up manner when the need to do so is real. Adult suggestions intended to direct that impulse into suitable channels are more useful than efforts to arouse that impulse. The nine-year-old boy who was solemnly told on the death of his father, by another member of the family, "You will look after your mother and your little sisters as your father would have done; you will have to stand by them," was not quite sure what the injunction to stand-by them entailed. As a result he dogged his mother's footsteps for days until she discovered this was his interpretation of stand-ing-by. He would naturally have stayed close to her during those days anyway, but the confusing admonition burdened him unnecessarily.

When death or divorce removes one parent from the home, the eldest will probably develop an especially close relationship with the parent who takes care of him. Either a father or a mother will tend to confide in his first child and talk over plans for the future with him more than he would have done under normal circumstances. This sharing can be a comforting support to both, without making the boy or girl feel he must replace the parent who is gone. To lean on an eldest, which is inevitable, does not mean to put the entire weight of the situation on him.

Any child can bear the truth better than he can bear being shut out. A parent does not need to feel his own worries must be constantly concealed. The boy or girl who knows his parent is troubled and understands why tends to be less disturbed and disturbing than the one whose parents attempt to maintain an unnatural cheeriness. Children need not be burdened with all the details, but they can know in a general way what is happening. They can also know the steps that are being taken to meet the difficulties and that provisions are being made for their family's care. A youngster who is given an honest picture of the situation the family faces may develop a sense of obligation to his family, but he can still be a child and not a pseudo-adult.

A helpful account of discussing death, divorce or lengthy separations with children can be found in *Parents Can be People* (N. Y., Appleton, 1944), by Dorothy W. Baruch, Chapter 11, and *Your Best Friends Are Your Children* (N. Y., Appleton, 1951), by Adele Franklin and Agnes Benedict, Chapter 9.

The family in which the mother is the remaining parent has been dealt with from three points of view in recent books. *Children of Divorce* (N. Y., Harper, 1953) by Louise Despert, M. D., deals chiefly with emotional problems a fatherless family faces. *Mothers On Their Own* (N. Y., Harper, 1953) by Ellen Rochford, takes up such practical questions as jobs and living arrangements. *Only Parent* (Phil., Lippincott, 1953) by Louise Dickinson Rich, is an account of the author's personal experiences.

A father left with several children is more helpless than a mother. Even economically he is at a comparable disadvantage if he must add to his budget the cost of someone to clean, cook, wash, mend, and look after his children. He may depend on his eldest daughter, if he has one, for practical assistance to a greater extent than a mother does on a son. The eldest daughter, if she is more than nine or ten, is expected to know what her mother would have done and in some cases to carry out her mother's practices.

An eldest son in a motherless family might also be required to carry responsibilities for housekeeping, shopping, and keeping younger children in line. His father might treat him as a partner in managing the family and talking over problems with him. Yet for a boy this situation would be a temporary one, while for a girl, it would be the pattern that she would follow throughout her life.

The girl may be permanently caught, or choose to remain, in this position. During her adolescence she may find great satisfaction in taking her mother's place. She may cheerfully insist on renouncing educational opportunities, and much of the usual social life of the teen-ager because of a genuine devotion to her father. She may pride herself on the position she holds with her father, for girls in their teens are likely to feel affection for a father similar to what they had ten or twelve years earlier.

It might be better if such a girl were encouraged to go ahead with her own life and continue her associations with her contemporaries. Her father needs friends of his own, but in the face of his daughter's sacrifices he may hesitate to look for company among his old friends, much less seek new ones or select a second wife. If her father can let her feel that he is not dependent on her company or her care, she is less likely to center her goals around replacing her mother.

An only parent needs to keep in mind that the eldest will act his age, sometimes in surprising ways, no matter how sensible and reliable he may appear to be. A high school girl, who since her mother's death had behaved with remarkable maturity toward her younger sisters and toward the responsibilities imposed on her, insisted her father go shopping with her for a party dress. The father thought the shopping expedition had been a great success and congratulated himself on having expressed no opinion until he was asked. Even then he had encouraged his daughter to make her own choice. He was dismayed to overhear her say to a friend later, "I'm not so crazy for what I got, but you know what parents are—always wanting you to buy the wrong thing." Mothers, of course, are more accustomed to such responses and do not take them quite so seriously. There spoke the confusion of the adolescent who wants to be told what to do so that he can prove his independence by rebelling against parental directives.

The mother who is left alone may not find an eldest son or daughter rallying to the cause with quite so much fervor as is displayed when a father is the only parent. The loss of a mother causes drastic changes in the daily life of the family. The eldest must perforce take steps to keep routines going if he is old enough to do so. In the absence of the father, even though a mother must take a job outside her home, meals, perhaps slimmer ones, are still put on the table. Clothes, though perhaps old and patched, are still washed and ironed. Yet without a father's daily departure and return, life lacks pattern and interest. A mother, who bears the brunt of an eldest's resentment, is likely to find that her first child does not always assume his burdens cheerfully or heroically.

THE WELL-TEMPERED STEPMOTHER

There is a tendency to blame the stories about the wicked stepmother for the ill-repute of these maligned women. The preposterous suggeston has even been put forward that tales like "Snow White" and "Cinderella" should be banned or rewritten so that the child who acquired a stepparent would not bring prejudices to the situation. This would be as futile as it would be impossible. The real cause of the dubious reputation of the stepmother goes deeper and has nothing to do with the behavior of any stepmother, living or dead. Like the adopted child, the stepchild feels whenever he is disappointed, "My own mother would never do this." The stories are the result, not the cause, of the universal desire to be cared for and indulged.

A child's age when a stepparent enters his life influences the relationship between the two. Given a kindly, understanding person, a young child is likely to form an attachment more readily than one who is older. From the point of view of a boy or girl between twelve and fifteen, there is more to be lost and less to be gained in acquiring a stepparent than in the earlier years. A small child may make his protest, if he has one to make, in words or by acting angry. An older one may refrain from open conflict, but his antagonism can be felt in subtle ways.

Stepparents have been thoroughly discussed from the sociological point of view in *The Stepchild* (Chicago, University of Chicago Press, 1953), by William Carlson Smith. *Stepmothers Can Be Nice* (Public Affairs Pamphlets No. 198), by Helen Steers Burgess, presents a practical approach.

The eldest of several children whose parent remarries is likely to have a clearer memory of the parent lost through death or divorce and of the household headed by his own mother and father than do his younger brothers and sisters. Idealized memories, his closeness to the remaining parent during the one-parent period, plus the tendency to look nostalgically to the past make the new situation harder for him than for the younger members of the family. These attitudes also make dealing with the eldest more complicated for the stepparent.

When Mr. Dow asked his second wife to marry him, she was convinced she could in a few months transform the dingy Dow apartment and the four unkempt children into something trimmer, brighter, and more agreeable. The second Mrs. Dow valued crispness and efficiency—qualities that had never been strong points with her predecessor. The stepmother undertook her new duties with good will and enthusiasm. She had become well enough acquainted with the children before her marriage to feel at ease with the three younger ones. The greater reserve of Joan, the eldest, she attributed to the girl's having grown old before her time as the manager of the household.

Joan identified herself with her mother to such an extent that she regarded her father's remarriage as an act of disloyalty not merely to her mother's memory, but to herself. Much as she had missed her mother, she had found being deferred to by the other children, consulted by her father, and freedom to do as she pleased a highly satisfactory way of life.

Like many adolescents, Joan had a fine sense of the dramatic. Before the wedding she called the children to her and solemnly told them that she was sure their father's new wife meant well and would do her best. Still they must remember how remarkable their own mother had been and how bravely she had endured her last illness. She, Joan, would never forget what their mother had taught her and she hoped the younger ones would follow those teachings. Joan's speech was probably the neatest piece of subversion since Anthony's address in *Julius Caesar*.

Joan was not openly rebellious to her stepmother. She merely ignored her and subtly encouraged the younger children to do the same. Mr. Dow found himself caught between Joan and his wife, each of whom was doing the right thing according to the dictates of her conscience and each of whom was miserably unhappy. The numerous changes in decor, menus, and routines instituted by his second wife were an improvement over Joan's sketchy housekeeping in Mr. Dow's opinion, but he could not tell his daughter that.

The climax came when Joan tried to run away from home. Then Mrs. Dow realized the problem was one she could not solve alone. She consulted the local family welfare society. Her interviews with the case worker there helped her understand that even though she was acting from the best of motives she had moved too fast in bringing about innovations. She saw more clearly what it means to a proud and sensitive adolescent to have her achievements repudiated. Joan and her stepmother never were able to reach the friendly footing Mrs. Dow eventually established with the younger children.

When a stepmother comes into a home that has been motherless for some time she is likely to find a slackness that seems to need correcting. If she appreciates what the eldest has done or feels she has done in holding the family together and waits to make changes until she has made friends, she will meet less antagonism. If the oldest girl is given a well-defined, rewarding part to play so that she maintains her prestige with the younger children, the girl will feel less pushed aside. Encouraging her to talk about her own mother, or showing interest in the former customs of the household, is not easy, but the result may be less mistrust on the part of the eldest, and a better relationship with all the children.

The course events took in the Dow household is not the only possible pattern. Some eldest daughters might be pleased to be relieved of their responsibilities and welcome a woman who would give them a cheerful, well-run home. Others might be able to voice their objections instead of letting their annoyance pile up inside as it did in Joan's case. Coming to terms with the hopes and fears of adolescence plus a stepmother presents a double problem and accounts for some of Joan's bitterness.

ONLY CHILD INTO STEPCHILD

He who has been an only child and then becomes the eldest among stepbrothers and sisters has a different set of problems. The change from having had a mother or father entirely to oneself and then being required to accept a stepparent often appears to be a further loss instead of a gain. The child who has shared a room with his parent and then must relinquish that place to the new member of the family finds it hard to accept the new regime.

When another child is born who belongs to both parents, the stepchild has good grounds for fearing that he will be the outsider. If it is his mother who has remarried, the new baby will bear the parents' name, while he does not. Here is both a practical and an emotional hazard. This has been satisfactorily resolved in some cases by the stepfather's legal adoption of his wife's child by her first marriage. In other cases the child has taken the stepfather's name without legal adoption to simplify daily life. Occasionally, the child's own father's family object on sentimental grounds to such a change, but it is an objection that should not carry too much weight, for this difference in name can become a sensitive point for a growing child.

An adolescent girl who was fond of her stepfather and had never complained before, became distressed when she entered high school because she was, she claimed, "just nobody at all, not even anywhere in the phone book." Her half-sisters, she said, were the only ones who counted. They had more dates even though they were younger and it was all because nobody could find her. This was the real problem of the adolescent and her dates. Her feeling that she didn't exist because her name wasn't in the telephone book symbolized this adolescent's search for herself. When her stepfather gave her, as a birthday present, a listing under her own name in the telephone book, he was not just indulging her whims. He was proving to her symbolically that she was a person in her own right.

Some stepparents, like some adopting parents and for similar reasons, may find it easier to be forgiving and tolerant with a stepchild. Their standards for the stepchild may not be as high and they do not feel as deeply involved when he falls short in some way as they do when their own son or daughter makes a mistake. There is as a result a paradoxical closeness brought about by the distance between stepparent and stepchild.

STEPBROTHERS AND SISTERS CAN BE FRIENDS

In the same way, a friendship can spring up between children brought together by the marriage of their parents. If the marriage has been welcomed by both groups of children, and they prove congenial, the eldest may have less resentment toward these youngsters with whom he has no blood ties than he has toward the younger offspring of his own parents. When a child is born of this marriage he may become a protege rather than a rival of the eldest, if that one has found the stepparent agreeable and the new arrangement appears to have advantages for him.

Whether an eldest responds to his new life with a stepparent by open resistance, retreating into fantasies, conforming outwardly, running away, or working out a sensible compromise, or whether he uses some combinations of these responses will depend on what the remarriage of his parent has meant to him. Not only the treatment the stepparent gives him, but what he feels he has gained or lost by the new arrangement influences his feelings. For the eldest who has consciously or unconsciously looked back on not having to share his parent as a happy state, this new sharing may seem harder and he may adjust to it less well than the other children in the family.

THE PSEUDO-ELDEST

A child born after his parents have lost another has an amorphous position. Unlike a real eldest child, he is not the prototype for his parents. The child whom they lost is the model with whom he is compared. Perhaps they want him to be like that one, or they may be afraid when they see a resemblance that it presages an untimely end for this one, too. When a second child becomes eldest in a family he is likely to undergo more of the disadvantages and reap fewer gains than usually accrue to a first-born.

Most of us go through life believing that the worst will not happen. When tragedy does occur, we lose that buoyant self-confidence and become apprehensive even when the facts do not warrant it. Parents who have lost a child tend to be understandably anxious and overprotective at least about matters in any way connected with the first child's death.

A boy or girl should know about the child who died even though he has no memory of him. The price of a hush-hush atmosphere about an event of such importance will be greater than the inconvenience of answering questions about death.

Sometimes a child may feel, "They only wanted me to take the place of the one they lost," or "I'm not what they wanted. I'm not as good as my brother would have been." Here again is a convenient hook on which to hang self-doubts or resentment when life is hard. Knowing that there was another child in the family does not in itself create these doubts although it may give them a different expression than they would otherwise have had. Children often feel the same way about a living brother or sister. Since the living one makes mistakes from time to time, he is less competition than one whose failings are unknown and whose virtues may be exaggerated. Parents can take care not to let the child whom they lost loom large on the horizon of the one who follows him. Above all, they can avoid making comparisons between the two or saying "You were sent to us to take his place."

This is another instance of the need for each individual to be allowed to be himself rather than take the place of another, for that can only result in confusion and frustration.

WHEN A YOUNGER CHILD DIES

Child mortality has been so greatly reduced that the loss of a brother or sister is an unusual circumstance for a child to experience today in the United States. Since adults no longer are resigned to such loss, and since the eldest does not see other families similarly stricken, the death of a younger brother or sister is far more shocking to a child than it would have been in an earlier day.

Children have a faulty notion of cause and effect and an exaggerated idea of their own power. An eldest who may often have wished a brother or sister out of the way may feel his wishes have contributed to the death. This feeling is reinforced if a child knows his parents blame themselves for what has happened.

A child can be allowed but not forced to talk about his feelings. Sometimes it is easier for him to express what is on his mind if his mother or father says, "When I was small, I believed . . ." He can be reassured that his thoughts and wishes, even his words, have no effect on events. Such reassurance is best given indirectly, for if it appears that adults are mind readers, a child's belief in baleful magic is strengthened.

If a child in the family dies, parents may attempt to hide their grief from the other children. One mother who did that found her eldest showing signs of real disturbance. When the mother, in spite of herself, gave way to tears in the presence of the eldest one day, this seven-year-old exclaimed with relief, "Oh, then you really did love the baby. I was afraid you didn't love him because you never cried, and you wouldn't have cried if I had died either." This situation has arisen often enough to be convincing proof once more that only emotional honesty on the part of parents can maintain emotional well-being in the children.

BY WAY OF SUMMING UP

To be the eldest can have many meanings. Feelings about that position range from those expressed by Toni in G. B. Stern's *The Matriarch* (N. Y., Knopf, 1925), "I shall always do just as I like and knock down everybody, and everybody will love me best, because I'm the oldest of the oldest of the oldest," to that expressed by the hero of Arthur Koestler's *Arrival and Departure* (N. Y., Macmillan, 1943), "They were always fussing around that creature, and I was pushed aside. Yes, I must have hated it with all my heart . . . Had they not neglected me for the sake of the other—the spoiled, the pampered one, the tyrannic little monster?"

The wide variety of behavior among eldest children discussed in this book is only a sampling, but it demonstrates that how the situation is handled, not the position itself, influences personality. To parents and teachers who reduce the trials of the position and highlight its advantages, who make the privileges as well as the responsibilities of seniority evident, can come this gratifying tribute: If a child seems comfortable in playing his part as eldest, and likes himself, the adults who live with him can be proud of themselves and of this first-born.

APPENDIX I

References Used in the Preparation of Chapter I, "Myth and Custom of the Eldest"

Asbjornsen, Peter Christen, *East of the Sun and West of the Moon* (edited by Ingri and Edgar P. d'Aulaire), N. Y., Viking Press, 1938.

Bacon, Elizabeth Emaline, *The Hazara Mongols: A Study in Social Organization* (dissertation submitted in partial satisfaction of the degree of Ph.D. in anthropology, Graduate Division of the University of California, August 1951).

Beaglehole, Ernest and Pearl, *Personality Development in Pukapukan Children* (Language, Culture and Personality, edited by Leslie Spier, H. Irving Hallowell, Stanley S. Newman, Menasha, Wis., Sapir Memorial Publications Fund, 1941).

Benet, Sula, *Song, Dance and Customs of Peasant Poland*, N. Y., Roy Publishers, 1951.

Braeksted, H. L., *Fairy Tales from the Swedish of G. Djurklo*, N. Y., Stokes, 1901.

Brant, Charles, *Tadagale: A Burmese Village in 1950* (Cornell University Southeast Asia Program, Data Paper #13, Ithaca, 1954).

Carpenter, Frances, *Tales of A Chinese Grandmother*, Garden City, N. Y., Doubleday, 1938.

———, *Tales of A Korean Grandmother*, Garden City, N. Y., Doubleday, 1947.

————, *Tales of A Swiss Grandmother*, Garden City, N. Y., Doubleday, 1949.

————, *Tales of A Russian Grandmother*, Garden City, N. Y., Doubleday, 1933.

Cervin, Vladimir, "Problems in the Integration of the Afghan Nation," *The Middle East Journal*, Vol. 6:400-416, Washington, D. C., 1952.

Colum, Padriac, *Legends of Hawaii*, New Haven, Yale University Press, 1937.

————, *The Arabian Nights*, N. Y., Macmillan, 1923.

Downes, R. M., *The Tiv Tribe*, Kaduna, The Government Printer, 1933.

Encyclopedia of the Social Sciences, edited by Edwin Seligman, N. Y., Macmillan, 1953.

Enjoy, Paul d', "La Famille Annamite," *Revue Scientifique*, Series 4, Vol. 5:243-244, Paris, Bureau des Revues, 1896.

Firth, Raymond, *We, The Tikopia, A Sociological Study of Kinship in Primitive Polynesia*, London, Allen and Unwin, 1936.

Fortes, Meyer, "Kinship and Marriage among the Ashanti," *African Systems of Kinship and Marriage*, edited by Radcliffe Brown, A. R., and Forde, D., London, Oxford University Press, for the International African Institute, 1950.

Foster, James R., *Great Folk Tales of Wit and Humor*, N. Y., Harper & Brothers, 1955.

————, *The World's Great Folk Tales*, N. Y., Harper & Brothers, 1953.

Frazer, Sir James George, *The Golden Bough*, Vol. 4, N. Y., Macmillan, 1935.

Fried, Morton H., *Fabric of Chinese Society*, N. Y., Frederick A. Praeger, 1953.

Grierson, Elizabeth Wilson, *Scottish Fairy Book*, N. Y., Stokes, 1910.

Griffis, William Elliot, *Corea: The Hermit Nation*, N.Y., Charles Scribner's Sons, 1882.

Henry, William E., "The Thematic Apperception Technique in

the Study of Culture," *Genetic Psychology Monograph,* Vol. XXLV: 103-135, Provincetown Journal Press, 1947.

Hewes, Gordon W., & Kim, Chin Hong, *Korean Kinship Behavior and Structure,* unpublished mss., 1950.

Hulbert, Homer B., "The Status of Women in Korea," *The Korean Review,* Vol. II, Seoul, Methodist Publishing House, 1902.

Hutereau, Armand, "Notes Sur La Vie Familiale et Juridique de Quelque Populations du Congo Belge," *Annales du Musée du Congo Belge, Ethnographie et Anthropologie,* Ser. 3: Documents Ethnographiques Concernant Les Populations du Congo Belge, Vol. I, Pt. 1, Bruxelles: Ministre des Colonies, 1909.

Jacobs, Joseph, *English Fairy Tales,* N.Y., G. P. Putnam's Sons, 1902.

————, *Indian Fairy Tales,* N.Y., G. P. Putnam's Sons, 1892.

Junod, Henri, *Thonga, Life of A South African Tribe,* Vol. II, London, Macmillan, 1927.

Karve, Irawati, "Kinship Organization in India," *Deccan College Monograph Series,* Poona, 1953.

Kluckhohn, Clyde, "Navaho Witchcraft," *Papers of the Peabody Museum of American Archaelogy and Ethnology,* Cambridge, Harvard University Press, Vol. XXII, #2, 1944.

————, "Some Aspects of Navaho Infancy and Early Childhood," *Psychoanalysis and the Social Sciences,* Vol. I, N. Y., International University Press, 1947.

————, and Leighton, Dorothea, *The Navaho,* Cambridge, Harvard University Press, 1946.

Lang, Olga, *Chinese Family and Society,* New Haven, Yale University Press, 1946.

Levette, J., *A Guide to American Folklore,* Denver, University of Denver Press, 1951.

Levy, Marion J., *The Family Revolution in Modern China,* Cambridge, Harvard University Press, 1949.

Lowre, Robert H., *The Crow Indians,* N. Y., Farrar and Rinehart, 1935.

"The Lapps," *Indiana University Subcontractors Monograph,*

Human Relations Area File - 3, Indiana - 6, prepared for Human Relations Area File in 1955 in typescript.

Macculoch, J. A., *Childhood of Fiction*, London, John Murray, 1905.

Mandelbaum, David G., "The Family in India," *Southwestern Journal of Anthropology*, Vol. 4, Albuquerque, University of New Mexico Press, 1948.

Mathews, Washington, "The Study of Ethics Among the Lower Races," *Journal of American Folklore*, Vol. XII, Boston, Houghton Mifflin, 1899.

Mi Mi Khaing, *Burmese Family*, Calcutta, Longmans, 1946.

Moose, J. Robert, *Village Life in Korea*, Nashville, Methodist Episcopal Church, 1911.

Morgan, Edward, *The Birth of the Republic: The Chicago History of American Civilization Series*, edited by Daniel Boorstin, Chicago, University of Chicago Press, 1956.

Paul, Benjamin D., "Sibling Rivalry in A Guatemalan Village," *American Anthropologist*, Vol. 52, 1950.

Perrault, Charles, *Puss in Boots*, N. Y., Charles Scribner's Sons, 1952.

Plaut, Hermann, "Beitrage zur Kenntniss der Insel Formosa," *Mittheihungen des Seminars fur Orientalische Sprachen*, Vol. VI, Berlin, Georg Reimer, 1903.

Osgood, Cornelius, *The Koreans and Their Culture*, N. Y., The Ronald Press, 1951.

Raum, O. F., *Chaga Childhood: A Description of Indigenous Education in An East African Tribe*, London, Oxford University Press for International Institute of African Language and Cultures, 1940.

Reichard, Gladys A., *Navaho Religion, A Study in Symbolism*, N. Y., Bollingen Foundation, Vol. I., 1950.

Rockhill, W. Woodville, "Notes on Some of the Laws, Customs and Superstitions of Korea," *American Anthropologist*, Vol. IV, Washington, Anthropological Society of Washington, 1891.

Sanders, Irwin T., *Balkan Village*, Lexington, The University of Kentucky Press, 1949.

Seligman, Charles Gabriel, and Seligman, Bernard G., *Pagan Tribes of the Nilotic Sudan*, London, Geo. Routledge and Sons, 1932.

Simmonds, Donald Charles, *The Alamo Navaho Kinship and Sibling System*, unpublished mss.: Master's Thesis, Yale University, 1950.

Spiro, Melford E. A., *Ifaluk; A South Sea Culture*, unpublished mss., submitted as A Final Report, Coordinated Investigation of Micronesian Anthropology, Washington, Pacific Science Board, National Research Council, 1949.

Stevenson, Margaret, *The Rites of the Twice Born*, London, Oxford University Press, 1920.

Strehlow, Theodor Georg Heinrich, *Aranda Traditions*, Carlton, Melbourne University Press, 1947.

Thorner, Daniel and Thorner, Alice, *India and Pakistan*, in *Most of the World*, edited by Ralph Linton, N. Y., Columbia University Press, 1949.

Bibliography of Materials on the Eldest Child

Aarons, Z. Alexander, "Effect of the Birth of A Sister on A Boy in His Fourth Year," *Psycho-analytic Quarterly*, Vol. 22, No. 3, 1953.

Abernathy, E. M., "Data on Personality and Family Position," *Journal of Psychology*, Vol. 10:303-307, 1940.

Ackerman, Nathan W., "Reciprocal Antagonism in Siblings," *Bulletin of Menninger Clinic*, Vol. 2:1, 1938.

Adler, Alfred, "Character of First, Second and Third Children," *Children*, Vol. 3:14-52, 1928.

Anon., "Ambivalence in First Reaction to Sibling Rivalry," *Journal of Abnormal Psychology*, Vol. 44, 1949.

Bakan, David, "Relationship of Alcoholism and Birth Rank," *Quarterly Journal of Studies on Alcohol*, Vol. 10:434-440, 1949.

Becker, Mildred, "Effect of Activity Group Therapy on Sibling Rivalry," *Smith College Studies in Social Work*, Vol. 16:131-132, 1945.

Benedek, Therese, "Emotional Structure of the Family," in *The Family, Its Function and Its Destiny*, edited by Ruth Nanda Anshen, N. Y., Harper & Brothers, 1949.

Blanchard, Phyllis, "Psycho-analytic Contributions to the Problem of Reading Difficulties," *Psycho-analytic Study of the Child*, Vol. II, N. Y., International Universities Press, 1946.

Bonney, M. E., "A Study of the Relation of Intelligence, Family

Size and Sex Difference to Mutual Friendship in Primary Grades," *Child Development*, Vol. 13:79-100, 1942.

———, "Relationship Between Social Success, Family Size, Socio-economic Home Background and Intelligence among School Children," *Sociometry*, Vol. 7:26-39, 1944.

Bossard, James H. S., Sociology of Child Development, N. Y., Harper & Brothers, 1947.

———, *The Large Family System*, Phila., University of Pennsylvania Press, 1956.

Boyce, L. Bryce, "Christmas 'Neurosis'," *Journal of American Psycho-analytic Association*, Vol. 3:467, 1955.

Bramwell, B. S., "The Order of Merit: The Holders and Their Kindred," *Eugenics Review*, Vol. 36:84-91,1944.

Cahn, Paulette, "L'Enfant Ainé," *L'Ecole Des Parents et Des Educateurs*, Paris, France. (n.d.)

———, "Le Role du Jeu dans l'Evolution de la Relation Fraternelle d'un Ainé," *Sauvegarde*, Vol. 4:40-52, 1949.

———, "Quand Freres et Soeurs Se Disputent," *L'Ecole Des Parents et Des Educateurs*, Paris, France. (n.d.)

Cattell, J. McK., *American Men of Science*, Garrison, N. Y., Science Press, 1927.

Child Study Magazine, Spring, 1950.

Cobb, Stanley, and McDermott, Neil T., "A Psychological Survey of 50 Cases of Bronchial Asthma," *Psychosomatic Medicine*, Vol. I, #2, 1939.

Damrin, Dora E., "Family Size and Sibling Age, Sex and Position as Related to Certain Aspects of Adjustment," *Journal of Social Psychology*, Vol. 29:93-103, 1949.

Descombey, J., and Roquelbrune, G., "L'Enfant Characteriel parmi Ses Freres et Ses Soeurs," *Enfrance*, Vol. 6:329-368, 1953.

Elste, Ellen Anna, "Sibling Relationships Observed During Simultaneous Activities," *Clark University Bulletin, Abstracts of Dissertations and Theses*, Vol. 19, No. 182, 1947.

Fisher, Alfred, "Sibling Relations with Special Reference to

Problems of the Second Born," *Journal of Pediatrics,* Vol. 40:254-259, 1952.

Flugel, J. C., *Psycho-analytic Study of the Family,* London, Hogarth Press, 1947.

Galton, Francis, *English Men of Science: Their Nature and Nurture,* London, Macmillan, 1874.

Gates, Mary Frances, "A Comparative Study of Some Problems of Social and Emotional Adjustment of Crippled and Non-Crippled Girls and Boys," *Journal of Genetic Psychology,* Vol. 68:219-244, 1946.

Gottemoeller, Ruth, "Sibling Relationships of Groups of Young Children," *The Nervous Child,* Vol. 2, 1943.

Haag, F. E., "Untersuchungen über Allerzischen Krankheiten die Stellung des Allergisch Erkrankten in der Geschwisterreih," *Klen. Wehnschr.,* Vol. 15:923-925, 1936.

Harris, Dale B., Clark, Kenneth E., Rose, Arnold M., and Valasek, Frances, "Measurement of Responsibility in Children," *Child Development,* Vol. 25, 1954.

————, "The Relationship of Children's Home Duties to an Attitude of Responsibility," *Child Development,* Vol. 25, 1954.

Hawkins, Mary O'Neil, "Jealousy and Rivalry in Brothers and Sisters," *Child Study,* Summer, 1946.

Henry, Jules and Zunia, "Symmetrical Reciprocal Hostility in Sibling Rivalry," *American Journal of Orthopsychiatry,* Vol. 12:256, 1942.

Hilgard, Josephine, "Sibling Rivalry and Social Heredity," *Psychiatry,* Vol. 14, #4, 1951.

Hsaio, H. A., "Status of First Born with Specific Reference to Intelligence," *Journal of Genetic Psychology,* Vol. 9:1-118, 1931.

Huet, G. J., "Asthma and the Order of Birth," *Nederlandsch Tijdschriftvoor Geneeskunde,* Vol. 47:3501-3507, 1955. (Resumé in English)

Jenkins, Richard L., and Thurstone, L. L., *Order of Birth, Parent Age and General Intelligence,* Chicago, University of Chicago Press, 1931.

Kalhorn, Joan, "Mental Test Performance of Siblings," *American Psychologist*, Vol. 13:265, 1948.

Karpman, Benjamin, "A Psychoanalytic Study of Fraternal Twins," *American Journal of Orthopsychiatry*, Vol. 21:735-755, 1951.

Kingsley, Alice, and Reynolds, Earle L., "The Relationship of Illness Patterns in Children to Ordinal Position in the Family," *Journal of Pediatrics*, Vol. 35:17-24, 1949.

Knickerbocker, Laura, "Treatment of Conflicts Arising in Sibling Rivalry," *Bulletin Menninger Clinic*, Vol. 4, #12, 1940.

Krishnan, B., "Order of Birth and Temperament," *Indian Journal of Psychology*, Vol. 26:85-87, 1951.

Koch, Helen L., "Attitudes of Young Children Toward Their Peers," *Psychological Monographs (General and Applied)*, Vol. 70, No. 19, No. 426, 1956.

———, "Children's Work Attitudes and Sibling Characteristics," *Child Development*, Vol. 27, No. 3, 1956.

———, "Relation of Certain Family Constellation Characteristics and Attitudes of Children Toward Adults," *Child Development*, Vol. 24, No. 1, 1955.

———, "Relationship of Primary Mental Abilities in Five and Six Year Olds to Sex of Child and Characteristics of His Siblings," *Child Development*, Vol. 25, No. 3, 1954.

———, "Sibling Influence on Children's Speech," *Journal of Speech and Hearing Disorders*, Vol. 21, No. 3, 1956.

———, "Sissiness and Tomboyishness in Relation to Sibling Characteristics," *Journal of Genetic Psychology*, Vol. 88:231, 1956.

———, "Some Personality Correlates of Sex, Sibling Position and Sex of Sibling Among Five and Six Year Old Children," *Genetic Psychology Monographs*, Vol. 52:3-50, 1955.

Kohler et Cosnier-Massiere, "Le Sentiment d'abandon Chez Les Aines de Familles Nombreuses," *L'Ecole des Parents*, Vol. 1:32-34, 1954.

Lasko, Joan Kalhorn, "Parent Behavior Toward First and Second

Children," *Genetic Psychology Monographs,* Vol. 49:97-134, 1954.

Lees, J. P., and Newsome, L. J., "Family or Sibship Position and Aspects of Juvenile Delinquency," *British Journal of Delinquency,* Vol. 5, No. 1, 1954.

Lees, J. P., "Social Mobility of A Group of Eldest Born and Intermediate Adult Males," *British Journal of Psychology (General Section),* Vol. XLIII, Part 3, 1952.

Le Moal, P., "Les Relations des Freres et des Soeurs," *L'Ecole des Parents,* No. 6, 1956.

Levy, David, "Hostility Patterns," *American Journal of Orthopsychiatry,* Vol. 13, 1943.

———, *"Studies in Sibling Rivalry,"* N.Y., American Psychiatric Society, 1937.

Liss, Edward, "Coercion as A Factor in Sibling Rivalry," *Nervous Child,* Vol. 5, No. 3, 1946.

Luppono, A., "Relative Success in Treating Two Children in Same Family," *Smith College Studies in Social Work,* Vol. 16: 135-163, 1945.

Martin, Alexander Reid, *The Oldest and the Youngest Child* (summary of a lecture given before the auxiliary council to the Association for the Advancement of Psycho-analysis, N.Y., 1945).

Mead, Margaret, and Wolfenstein, Martha, *Childhood in Contemporary Cultures,* Chicago, University of Chicago Press, 1955.

Mead, Margaret, "Character Formation in Two South Sea Societies." *Transactions of American Neurological Society,* Vol. 68, 1950.

Montagu, Ashley, "Sex, Order of Birth and Personality," *American Journal of Orthopsychiatry,* Vol. 18:351, 1948.

Mauco, Georges et Rambaud, Paule, "Le Range de l'Enfant dans la Famille," *Revue Francaise de Psychanalyse,* Tome XV, No. 2:253-260, 1951.

Murphy, Lois B., "Emotional First Aid for Children," *Childhood Education,* 32:5, Jan. 1956.

Obendorf, Clarence P., "Psycho-analysis of Siblings," *American Journal of Psychiatry*, Vol. 8: No. 6, 1929.

Romm, May E., "The Unconscious Need to be an Only Child," *Psychoanalytic Quarterly*, Vol. 24:331, 1955.

Schoonover, S. K. M., "Sibling Resemblance in Achievement," *Dissertation Abstracts for Ph.D.*, University of Michigan, 1953.

Sears, Robert R., "Ordinal Position in the Family As A Psychological Variable," *American Sociological Review*, Vol. 15:397-401, 1950.

Sletto, Raymond F., "Sibling Position and Juvenile Delinquency," *American Journal of Sociology*, Vol. 39, No. 5, 1934.

Stedman, Jane Wheeler, "Comparison Between More Gifted and Less Gifted Siblings on Certain Personality Traits," *Clark University Bulletin, Abstracts of Dissertations and Theses*, Vol. 17, No. 74, 1945.

Stewart, Robert R., "Maladjustment and Reading Achievement," *American Journal of Orthopsychiatry*, Vol. 20, 1950.

Strauss, Bernard N., "The Dynamics of Ordinal Position Affects," *Quarterly Journal of Child Behavior*, Vol. 3, 1951.

Vollmer, H., "Jealousy in Children," *American Journal of Orthopsychiatry*, Vol. 16:660-771, 1946.

Wile, I. S., and Jones, A. B., "Ordinal Position and Behavior of Young Children," *Journal of Genetic Psychology*, Vol. 51:6, 1954.

Wolfenstein, Martha, "Analysis of a Juvenile Poem," *The Psycho-analytic Study of the Child*, N. Y., International Universities Press, Vol. XI, 450-470, 1956.

Wood, Mildred L., "Family Relations in Homes Containing Subnormal Child and Sibling," *Smith College Studies in Social Work*, Vol. 13, 1942.

UNPUBLISHED THESES

Cash, Audrey Sutton, *An Investigation of Reactions of High School Students Toward Certain Problem Situations Involving Younger Siblings*, Athens, University of Georgia, Graduate School, 1950.

Dean, Daphne A., *The Relation of Ordinal Position to Personality in Young Children,* Iowa City, unpublished master's thesis, State University of Iowa, 1947.

Levine, Joyce, *Effect of Psychiatric Hospitalization of Children Upon Their Siblings,* N.Y., New York School of Social Work, 1952.

King, Stanley, *Some Factors Related to Group Acceptance of Day Camp Children,* St. Louis, master's thesis, George Warren Brown, School of Social Work, Washington University, 1949.

APPENDIX III

Reading List for Parents

Baruch, Dorothy W., *Parents Can Be People*, N.Y., Appleton-Century-Crofts, 1944, Chapter 7.

Bossard, James H. S. and Boll, Eleanor Stoker, *The Large Family System*, Phila., University of Pennsylvania Press, 1956.

Buxbaum, Edith, *Your Child Makes Sense*, N.Y., International Universities Press, 1949. Chapter six.

Frank, Lawrence and Mary, *How to Help Your Child in School*, N.Y., The Viking Press, 1950. See index *Teasing* and *Six and Sevens*.

——, *Your Adolescent at Home and In School*, N.Y., The Viking Press, 1956, Chapter 8.

Gruenberg, Sidonie M., *We, The Parents*, N.Y., Harper & Brothers, 1948, Chapter III.

Josselyn, Irene M., M.D., *The Happy Child*, N.Y., Random House, 1955, Part V, 26.

Isaacs, Susan, *Troubles of Children and Parents*, London, Methuen, 1948, Chapter 6.

Neisser, Edith G., *Brothers and Sisters*, N.Y., Harper & Brothers, 1951.

Wolf, Anna M., *A Parent's Manual*, N.Y., Simon and Schuster, 1941, Chapter 4.

PAMPHLETS

Children in the Family, Rivals and Friends, Neisser, Edith G., N.Y., Teacher's College, 1951, available from Association for Family Living, 28 East Jackson Blvd., Chicago. 60¢.

Helping Brothers and Sisters Get Along, Puner, Helen W.,
Chicago, Science Research Associates, 1952, available from the
publisher, 57 W. Grand Ave., Chicago. 50¢.

Jealousy and Rivalry in Children, Reprint from *Child Study
Magazine,* 1946, available from Child Study Association of
America, 132 East 74th St., N.Y., or Association for Family
Living, 28 East Jackson St., Chicago. 25¢.

What Are the Causes of Sibling Conflict? Frank, Mary and Lawrence K., available from the Association for Family Living, 28
East Jackson St., Chicago. 5¢.

Getting Along with Brothers and Sisters, Ullmann, Frances,
Chicago, Science Research Associates, 1951, available from
Association for Family Living, 28 East Jackson St., Chicago.
50¢.

APPENDIX IV

The Eldest in Fiction, Drama, and Biography

(The following list is suggestive rather than exhaustive, and will perhaps lead the reader to discover other plays and novels in which the first-born is a central character.)

Austen, Jane, *Persuasion*, N.Y., Grove Press, 1949
———, *Pride and Prejudice*, N.Y., Grove Press, 1950
Bennett, Arnold, *Old Wives' Tale*, N.Y., Doubleday & Co., 1945
Butler, Samuel, *Way of All Flesh*, N.Y., Harper & Brothers, 1950
Cary, Joyce, *House of Children*, N.Y., Harper & Brothers, 1956.
Cather, Willa, *O Pioneers!*, Boston, Houghton Mifflin, 1913
———, *Song of the Lark*, Boston, Houghton Mifflin, 1937
Church, Richard, *Over the Bridge*, N.Y., E. P. Dutton & Co., 1956
Dickens, Charles, *Martin Chuzzlewit*, N.Y., Grossett & Dunlap, 1935
Dostoyevsky, Feodor, *Brothers Karamazov*, N.Y., The Macmillan Co., 1937.
Eliot, George, *Mill on the Floss*, N.Y., Grove Press, 1951
Gaskell, Elizabeth, *Cranford*, London, The Macmillan Co., 1935
Gill, Brendan, *The Day the Money Stopped*, N.Y., Doubleday & Co., 1957
Goodrich, Frances and Albert Hackett, *Diary of Anne Frank*, N.Y., Random House, 1956

163

Howard, Sydney, *The Silver Cord*, (in Theater Guild Anthology), N.Y., Random House, 1936

Lawrence, D. H., *Sons and Lovers*, N.Y., Harper & Brothers, 1951

Lehman, Rosamond, *Invitation to the Waltz*, N.Y., Henry Holt, 1932

Mann, Thomas, *Buddenbrooks*, N.Y., Alfred A. Knopf, 1938

Miller, Arthur, *Death of A Salesman*, N.Y., The Viking Press, 1951

O'Hara, Mary, *My Friend Flicka*, Phila., J. B. Lippincott Co., 1941

O'Neill, Eugene, *Long Day's Journey into Night*, New Haven, Yale University Press, 1956

Salinger, J. D., *Catcher in the Rye*, Boston, Little, Brown & Co., 1951

Raverat, Gwen, *Period Piece*, N.Y., W. W. Norton & Co., 1953

Thackeray, William Makepeace, *The Newcombes*, London, The Macmillan Co., 1923

West, Rebecca, *The Fountain Overflows*, N.Y., Viking Press, 1956

The Eldest in Contemporary Children's Literature

("Y"—the book appeals chiefly to children under seven years of age.

"M"—the seven- to ten-year-olds will enjoy having the book read to them, or may be able to read it themselves.

"I"—a book for the ten- to twelve-year-olds.

"O"—a book for those over twelve years of age.)

Bannon, Laura, *Big Brother*, Chicago, Albert Whitman & Co., 1950 Y & M

Bauman, John, *Idaho Sprout*, N.Y., William Morrow & Co., 1950 O

Beim, Jerrold, *Across the Bridge*, N.Y., Harcourt Brace, 1951 O

———, *With Dad Alone*, N.Y., Harcourt Brace, 1954 I & O

Beim, Lorraine, *Hurry Back*, N.Y., Harcourt Brace, 1949 O

Benary, Margot, *The Ark*, N.Y., Harcourt Brace, 1953 O

———, *Rowan Farm*, N.Y., Harcourt Brace, 1954 O

Bishop, Claire Huchet, *The Five Chinese Brothers*, N.Y., Coward-McCann, 1938 Y

———, *Pancakes Paris*, N.Y., Viking Press, 1947 M & Y

Brown, Pamela, *Family Troupe*, N.Y., Harcourt Brace, 1953 O

Clearly, Beverly, *Beezuz and Ramona*, N.Y., William Morrow & Co., 1945 I

Clymer, Eleanor, *The Latch Key Club*, Phila., David McKay Co., 1949 O

———, *The Trolley Car Family*, Phila., David McKay Co., 1947 I

Coatsworth, Elizabeth, *House Boat Summer*, N.Y., The Macmillan Co., 1942 M

———, *The Captain's Daughter*, N.Y., The Macmillan Co., 1950 O

———, *The Littlest House*, N.Y., The Macmillan Co., 1940 M

———, *Thief Island*, N.Y., The Macmillan Co., 1943 I

Coleman, Pauline, *The Different One*, N.Y., Dodd, Mead & Co., 1955 O

Crawford, Marion, *The Little Princesses*, N.Y., Harcourt Brace, 1950 O

Credle, Ellis, *Down, Down the Mountain*, N.Y., Thomas Nelson & Sons, 1934 Y

Dalgliesh, Alice, *The Courage of Sarah Noble*, N.Y., Charles Scribner's Sons, 1954 I

———, *The Davenports and the Cherry Pie*, N.Y., Charles Scribner's Sons, 1949 O

Daringer, Helen, *Biggety Anne*, N.Y., Harcourt Brace, 1954 I

———, *Like A Lady*, N.Y., Harcourt Brace, 1955 O

———, *Mary Montgomery, Rebel*, N.Y., Harcourt Brace, 1948 O

———, *Stepsister Sally*, N.Y., Harcourt Brace, 1952 O

De Angeli, Marguerite, *Up the Hill*, N.Y., Doubleday & Co., 1942 O

Desmond, Alice Curtis, *Glamorous Dolly Madison*, N.Y., Dodd Mead & Co., 1946 O

Emery, Ann, *Mountain Laurel*, N.Y., G. P. Putnam's Sons, 1948 O

———, *Senior Year*, Phila., The Westminster Press, 1949 O

Enright, Elizabeth, *The Saturdays*, N.Y., Rinehart & Co., 1941 O

———, *Then There Were Five*, N.Y., Rinehart & Co., 1944 O

Fennimore, Stephan, *Bush Holiday*, N.Y., Doubleday & Co., 1949 O

Friedman, Frieda, *Carol from the Country*, N.Y., William Morrow & Co., 1950 O

Freirmood, Elizabeth H., *The Wabash Knows the Secret*, N.Y., Doubleday, 1951 O

Frost, Frances, *Windy Foot at the County Fair*, N.Y., Whittlesey House, 1947 I

Hader, Berta and Elmer, *Lost in the Zoo*, N.Y., The Macmillan Co., 1951 Y

Hawkins, Quail, *The Best Birthday*, N.Y., Doubleday & Co., 1954 Y & M

Haywood, Carolyn, *Betsy's Little Star*, N.Y., William Morrow & Co., 1950 M & Y

Heward, Constance, *Ameliaranne and the Green Umbrella*, N.Y., British Book Centre, 1920 Y

Hull, Eleanor, *Tumbleweed Boy*, N.Y., Friendship Press, 1949 I & O

Hunt, Mable Leigh, *Little Girl with Seven Names*, Phila., J. B. Lippincott & Co., 1936 M

Jones, Elizabeth Orton, *Maminka's Children*, N.Y., The Macmillan Co., 1940 M

Judson, Clara I., *They Came From France*, Boston, Houghton Mifflin, 1943 O

Lampman, Evelyn Sibley, *Elder Brother*, N.Y., Doubleday & Co., 1951 O

Lattimore, Eleanor, *Junior*, N.Y., Harcourt Brace, 1938 M

Lenski, Lois, *Blueberry Corners*, Phila., Stokes, 1950 M

————, *Cotton in My Sack*, Phila., J. B. Lippincott & Co., 1949 O

————, *Little Family*, N.Y., Doubleday & Co., 1932 Y

————, *On A Summer's Day*, London, Oxford University Press, 1953 Y

————, *Papa Small*, London, Oxford University Press, 1951 Y

————, *Texas Tomboy*, Phila., J. B. Lippincott, 1950 O

Lewiton, Mina, *Rachel*, N.Y., Franklin Watts, 1954 I

McCloskey, Robert, *One Morning in Maine*, N.Y., The Viking Press, 1952 Y

Mason, Miriam, *A Biography of Kate Douglas Wiggin*, Boston, Houghton Mifflin, 1952 O

————, *The Sugar Bush Family*, N.Y., The Macmillan Co., 1954 M

Medearis, Mary, *Big Doc's Girl*, Phila., J. B. Lippincott & Co., 1942 O

Moody, Ralph, *Little Britches,* N.Y., W. W. Norton & Co., 1950 O

Moore, Verdine and Conkling, Fleur, *Billy Between,* Phila., The Westminster Press, 1951 O

Murphy, Frances Salomon, *Ready-Made Family,* N.Y., Thomas Crowell Co., 1953 I

Peckham, Betty, *Tangle-Britches,* N.Y., Aladdin Books, 1954 I

Sayers, Frances Clark, *Tag-Along-Tooloo,* N.Y., The Viking Press, 1942 Y

Scott, Sally, *Judy's Baby,* N.Y., Harcourt Brace, 1948 M

Seymour, Halverson Alta, *Kaatje and the Christmas Compass,* N.Y., Mars, 1954 M

Simon, Charlie May, *Bright Morning,* N. Y., E. P. Dutton & Co., 1943 I

Streatfield, Noel, *Ballet Shoes,* N.Y., Random House, 1937 O

————, *Movie Shoes,* N.Y., Random House, 1940 O

Taylor, Sydney, *All-of-A-Kind Family,* Chicago, Follett Publishing Co., 1951 Y & M

Tunis, John R., *Keystone Kids,* N.Y., Harcourt Brace, 1943 O

Unnerstad, Edith, *The Sauce Pan Journey,* (Translated from the Swedish by James Harker.) N.Y., The Macmillan Co., 1951 I

Van Stockum, Hilda, *Cottage at Bantry Bay,* N.Y., The Viking Press, 1938 I

Wilder, Laura Ingalls, *Little House in the Big Woods,* N.Y., Harper & Co., 1932 M

————, *Little House on the Prairie,* N.Y., Harper & Brothers, 1935 M

————, *On the Banks of Plum Creek,* N.Y., Harper & Brothers, 1937 M

————, *Little Town on the Prairie,* N.Y., Harper & Brothers, 1941 I

————, *These Happy Golden Years,* N.Y., Harper & Brothers, 1943 O

Worth, Kathryn, *They Loved to Laugh,* N.Y., Doubleday & Co., 1942 O

Yates, Elizabeth, *Amos Fortune, Free Man,* N.Y., Aladdin Books, 1950 O

INDEX

problems, behavior, *see* behavior disturbances, competition, conflicts, quarrels, teasing
   emotional, *see* emotional problems, feelings
   reading, 122
   training in solving, 92, 98, 123
property, handed on to eldest, 6, 7
   conflicts over, 15, 89
puberty, 77
punishment, 21, 26, 82, 91
   in other cultures, 12
Pushmi-pullyu, 30
Puss-in-Boots, 16

quarrels, 8, 9, 81 ff., 92, 101, 133; *see also* conflicts, teasing
   avoiding, 83

Ralston, W. R. S., 16
Raverat, Gwen, 72
Raymond, Louise, 132
Reading Ladders for Human Relations, 124
reassurance, for troubled child, 58, 62, 63-65, 66, 78, 79, 90, 112, 113, 115, 120, 122, 147
regression, *see* backsliding
remarriage, of parent, 141-145; *see also* stepparent
resentment, 12, 13, 28, 45, 47, 55, 56, 61, 64, 68, 69, 81, 86, 88, 92, 93, 116, 133, 135, 141, 146; *see also* anger, rivalry
   on part of parents, 23
resourcefulness, 97, 99
responsibility, Chapter VI., 10 ff., 13, 18, 80, 116, 119 ff., 138, 139
Revolutionary War, 7
Rich, Louise Dickenson, 83, 139
rites, connected with firstborn, Chapter I.
   curing, 12
rivalry, 9, 50 ff., 62, 69, 70, 81, 85, 86, 119, 133; *see also* competition, conflict, jealousy, resentment
Rochford, Ellen, 139
role, 21, 79, 114; *see also* model
   for eldest stepchild, 143
   playing, 125
Rome, 5

Rondell, Florence, 132, 135
Room for One More, 135
Rose, Anna Perrot, 135
routines, 1, 2, 36
Rufus, *see* Only Parent
Russia, 5
Russian Fairy Tales, 16

Sabines, 5
sacrifice of firstborn, 4, 5
   on part of eldest, 63, 107, 140
Sailor off the Bremen, 67
Salinger, J. D., 18
Salt of the Earth, 18, 56
San Pedrola La Laguna, 12
school, 72, 86, 92, 101, Chapter VII; *see also* nursery school, high-school
   age child, *see* child, school-age
   grade, 110
Scott, Sally, 61
Scouts, *see* groups
self-reliance, *see* independence
selfishness, 41
seniority rights, Chapter I, 78, 90
separation, for children in same family, 78, 128
sex
   all of one, 80
   different combinations of in family, 74
   minority of one, 80-81
   preference for one, 19
   status due to, 3
   worries about, 54, 60
sharing, 41, 69; *see also* generosity
   rooms, 89
   of parent's problems, 138
Shane, Harold and Ruth, 49
Shinto, 8
Shaw, Irwin, 67, 125
showing-off, 52, 123
shyness, 41, 57; *see also* anxiety, sociability
Simon, Norma, 49
sleep, disturbances in, 57
Sly Mongoose, 17
Smith, William Carlson, 141
sociability, 41, 42, 127; *see also* companionship, friends, groups
sorcerer, eldest as, 11
Spartan, 5